THE REVISED VERSION
EDITED FOR THE USE OF SCHOOLS

THE

BOOKS OF HAGGAI
AND ZECHARIAH

THE

BOOKS OF HAGGAI
AND ZECHARIAH

BY

T. W. CRAFER, D.D.

Warden of the College of Greyladies and Professor
of Theology at Queen's College, London

CAMBRIDGE
AT THE UNIVERSITY PRESS
1920

CAMBRIDGE UNIVERSITY PRESS
Cambridge, New York, Melbourne, Madrid, Cape Town,
Singapore, São Paulo, Delhi, Tokyo, Mexico City

Cambridge University Press
The Edinburgh Building, Cambridge CB2 8RU, UK

Published in the United States of America by
Cambridge University Press, New York

www.cambridge.org
Information on this title: www.cambridge.org/9780521279437

First published 1920
First paperback edition 2011

A catalogue record for this publication is available from the British Library

ISBN 978-0-521-04242-0 Hardback
ISBN 978-0-521-27943-7 Paperback

PREFACE BY THE GENERAL EDITOR
FOR THE OLD TESTAMENT

THE aim of this series of commentaries is to explain the Revised Version for young students, and at the same time to present, in a simple form, the main results of the best scholarship of the day.

The General Editor has confined himself to supervision and suggestion. The writer is, in each case, responsible for the opinions expressed and for the treatment of particular passages.

A. H. M^CNEILE.

October, 1919.

CONTENTS

GENERAL INTRODUCTION

§ 1. THE CONDITION OF THE WORLD AND THE POSITION OF THE JEWS WHEN HAGGAI AND ZECHARIAH PROPHESIED.

In the year 586 B.C. the kingdom of Judah, which had survived the northern kingdom of Israel by a little more than a hundred years, was absorbed into the great Babylonian empire. Jerusalem fell after a long siege, and the last king, Zedekiah, was blinded and taken captive to Babylon, whither his predecessor Jehoiachin had already been removed in 597, along with the chief men of the city. The Babylonian king Nebuchadrezzar left his general Nebuzaradan to complete the destruction of the city, which he did by setting fire to the temple and the other large buildings (see 2 Kings xxv. 1–25).

For about forty years, until the year 537, the city remained waste, the national life was destroyed, and only the poorest remained in the surrounding villages. But the continuity of the nation was maintained in Babylon. Any temptation to mingle with alien populations as the years went on was removed by an unknown prophet, who uttered the glorious words of national hope which are contained in the fortieth and following chapters of the book of Isaiah. And he had good ground for his hope. For the downfall of the cruel Babylonian empire, which had removed them from their country, was plainly at hand. Cyrus king of Persia was winning one fresh land after another, and was felt to be an unconscious instrument in God's hands for the liberation of the Jews. The prophet speaks, in Jehovah's name, to 'Cyrus, whose right hand I have holden, to subdue nations before him....For Jacob my servant's sake, and Israel mine elect, I have even called thee by thy name' (Is. xlv. 1 and 4). The climax came in

539 when Cyrus captured Babylon, and two years later
he wisely reversed the policy of those whose empire he
inherited, and won the esteem of subject nations such as
the Jews by allowing them to return to their land. The
last words of 2 Chronicles and the first words of Ezra
give the decree whereby they were allowed to return to
Jerusalem for the express purpose of rebuilding the temple.
Ezra ii. records that over 42,000 availed themselves of
the permission, and in 536 they set up the altar of burnt-
offering and laid the foundation of the temple (Ezra iii.).
But hindrances of various kinds followed. The mixed
population of the land, whose request to help in the work
the Jews could not grant, became their enemies, and
succeeded in having the work stopped (Ezra iv.). Sixteen
years elapsed, and nothing more had been done, in spite
of the readiness of their two rulers, Zerubbabel the civil
ruler, a prince of the royal line, and Joshua, the high-priest.
The people had lost heart, and a series of bad seasons had
reduced them to want. It seemed obvious that the building
of the temple must be further postponed, and so God's
house was ignored, while they bestowed what labour they
could spare upon the beautifying of their own houses
(Hagg. i.). It seemed as if the object of their return would
never be fulfilled, and without their central place of
worship they would soon have become merged after all
in the nations around. But in the year 520 the situation
was saved by Haggai and Zechariah, and the voice of
prophecy induced them to begin the work at once and take
new encouragement for the future. Moreover, the civil
wars in the Persian empire revived the old prophetic
expectation that the might of the nations would be broken,
and that they would welcome a peace in which Jerusalem
was the centre and the temple the chief glory of the world.
Both prophets help to restore the national spirit by re-
peating this hope of a Messianic kingdom, which they
boldly connect with the immediate future, and with the
name of Zerubbabel himself. The details of their message

will be considered later; for the present it is sufficient
to quote the subsequent testimony of the book of Ezra.
' Then rose up Zerubbabel...and Jeshua, and began to
build the house of God which is at Jerusalem : and with
them were the prophets of God helping them' (Ezra v. 2).
The work did not proceed without some opposition on the
part of those outside, but the satisfactory effect of the
complaint of the local Persian governor to headquarters
was that the original decree of Cyrus was discovered.
Darius therefore made a new decree which actually assigned
a sum for the assistance of the temple, and in four years
it was completed and dedicated (Ezra v. and vi.). Zechariah
uttered further warnings and encouragements in the year
518, and the narrator does not forget that the builders
'prospered through the prophesying of Haggai the prophet
and Zechariah the son of Iddo' (Ezra vi. 14). The feast of
dedication was held in the last month of the year 516. It
is curious that no record is left concerning the half-century
which followed. But this long silence is the less unfortunate
because of the abundant light shed on the crisis which
preceded it, by the writings of the two prophets. Neither
Zerubbabel nor Joshua seems to have made any further
name for himself. Haggai and Zechariah stand out as the
heroes and patriots of the hour, who secured the worship
of the one true God, and the existence of their countrymen
as a 'chosen people.'

§ 2.   RECENT CRITICISM AND THE BOOKS OF HAGGAI AND ZECHARIAH.

A few points must be touched upon briefly.

(1) It has been called in question whether more than a
few Jews returned in 536. The real 'Return' may have been
in 520. Haggai's evidence that the temple was 'founded'
in the latter year is used to discredit the chronology
of the book of Ezra, which speaks of its foundations being
laid in 536, and has some very confused records of how
the delay took place (see Ezra iv.). For other ways of

explaining the difficulty, see p. 22. Others would deny
that it was to the returned exiles at all that the prophets appealed, but to those who stayed in Palestine.
That Haggai addressed 'the remnant of the people' has
been used to suggest that it was those who were left in the
land. But if the return was not recent, there was no
special reason why the prophets should mention it. See
note on Hagg. ii. 3.

(2)   The introduction of comments in narrative form in
both books (Hagg. i. 12–15 and Zech. vii. 2, 3), has led to
the suggestion that they formed part of an account of the
rebuilding of the temple, 'chronologically arranged and
probably edited by Zechariah.' Short as is the book of
Haggai, some would regard ii. 10–19 as an interpolation,
there being points of difference between it and the rest of
the book.

(3)   The point of criticism of supreme interest is with
regard to the book of Zechariah. It may be regarded as
now established beyond a doubt that only chs. i.–viii.
are from his pen. His work ends before ch. ix. as certainly
as does Isaiah's before ch. xl. of his book. We will post-
pone the discussion of this point for the present, and
set it forth in a special Introduction to chs. ix.–xiv. (see
pp. 75 ff.). Their historical setting, as far as it can be
gathered, will also be given there.

INTRODUCTION TO HAGGAI

§ I. THE PERSONALITY OF THE PROPHET.

Nothing more is known of Haggai than we may learn from his own words, and from the record found in the book of Ezra, which tells that it was with the help of Haggai and Zechariah that the returned exiles under Zerubbabel and Joshua, after sixteen years' delay, at length began, in the year 520 B.C., to rebuild the ruined temple. It is curious that we are not even told his father's name. Had he been a priest (as some have thought), or of a prophetic family, this would certainly have been the case. But, like Amos long before him (Amos vii. 14), he seems to have been a simple layman, whose heart God stirred to utter an appeal to his nation in a year of crisis. The form of the word, which means 'My feasts,' has led some to conjecture that it is not a proper name at all, but was merely given to the man who seized the opportunity when the people were keeping some of Jehovah's feast days, to give them a message from his Lord. At least there is a somewhat similar name among the prophets, for Malachi simply means 'my messenger,' and may have been given to an unnamed prophet owing to the occurrence of the phrase in his prophecy (Mal. iii. 1).

In the absence of other information, traditions have abounded concerning Haggai.. In the early Church he was thought to have been a priest, born in Babylon. Jewish tradition considers him to have been already an old man when he came back to Jerusalem, and with this agree those commentators who infer from his words about Solomon's temple that he had seen it himself before its destruction in 586. If that were so, it is no wonder that his prophetic activity did not continue beyond the year 520!

§ 2.   HAGGAI'S MESSAGE AND ITS EFFECT.

The prophet had only one object in view—to force his countrymen to build the temple.   This was no easy thing to do, after the first enthusiasm of the returned exiles had died down, and sixteen disappointing years had elapsed. That he succeeded in doing so, meant that he saved his nation as God's chosen people, and prevented them from lapsing into the idolatry of the nations which surrounded them.   They would certainly have done so without a temple as the centre of their worship and a constant incentive to be true to the glorious past, and the pure mono-theism of the Old Testament which was to lead to the fuller revelation of the New would have disappeared and become of none effect.   His message took the form of alternate warning and encouragement.   He used the opportunity of the adversity to which his people were reduced, to work on their feelings and turn their thoughts inward.   His favourite word is 'Consider.'   The rest he was content to leave to his fellow-prophet Zechariah.

He was a religious patriot.   But he was more, for he looked out on the world around, as the former prophets had done.   Isaiah could give a foreign policy to his people, and proved right in his assurance that the Assyrian empire might be ignored, for Jerusalem would not be taken. Haggai thought he could read equally well the signs of the times.   The world-upheaval which followed the death of the Persian king Cambyses in 521 seemed likely to shake human society to its foundations.   It was God's opportunity to regenerate and reconstruct society.   But the Jews must offer themselves, their city and their restored temple, to be part of the divine plan.   They were powerless themselves to crush the material might of the armed nations.   But the civil wars which rent the whole Persian empire seemed likely to effect this without either divine or human intervention. And if the Jews turned to God and His temple, why should not the nations outside do the same? So he recalls the old picture of the nations flocking to Jerusalem, as the centre of God's worship. It had been given by Isaiah (ii. 2) and Micah (iv. 1), and even then was probably the common stock of prophetic utterance. It was as far as the Jewish mind could go towards a missionary ideal. But the glorifying of the ruined temple is still in Haggai's mind; the Gentiles will bring their riches to help in beautifying it.

But his original appeal to the people probably owed its success to the two leaders with whose names he coupled it. Zerubbabel the civil ruler, and Joshua the high-priest, who figure so largely in Zechariah's visions, were the mainstay of Haggai as well. If they helped the prophets, it was because it was they who took the lead, while the prophets helped *them* by their spiritual propaganda (Ezr. v. 2). No wonder therefore that they were regarded as having the chief part to play in the new reconstruction of society. But in the pre-exilic prophets, a kingly personality had been foreshadowed, who should be God's representative. The Messianic hope was centred in a royal personage who should herald the kingdom of God and the reign of peace. Such a rôle had never been connected with the priesthood. Haggai therefore passes by Joshua, and centres his hope in Zerubbabel, the prince of the royal Davidic line. Hence his final message, addressed to Zerubbabel alone, making him the signet on the hand of Jehovah. But though this leader of the people might fulfil the immediate duty of rebuilding the temple, he yet might fail to rise to the further ideal of Messianic leadership. And indeed the expected opportunity never came to him. For, contrary to Haggai's expectation, Darius succeeded in restoring order in the chaos of the empire, and carrying it on with the same reliance on earthly might.

Did Haggai's promise therefore prove false? May it not rather be said that the fault lay with the turn of events, and possibly with the inability of Zerubbabel to respond? If in the peace which follows the recent world-war, there is no spiritual reconstruction of society, and things have settled down to be as they were, we shall not scoff at those prophets who pointed us to new ideals of regeneration while we were in the throes of war; we shall only lament that the opportunity is past, and that those who might have risen to it failed to do so.

Haggai's message still rings down the ages, and it must be acknowledged that it rings true. The worship of God must be definite, it must make a difference to the whole of life. The Church must not be a side-issue, but men's lives must be moulded according to the need to glorify God by its means. The secular and material things of the world must be viewed in relation to it, and to the God of all. Nations and individuals alike must seize the opportunities which God puts in their way, and in wider ways increase His glory and raise the standard of human life.

§ 3. HAGGAI'S THEOLOGY.

It has been the fashion to regard him as a mere copier of earlier prophetic utterances, a feeble imitator of his great predecessors. He is far more than that. His theology is in the background, for his purpose is wholly practical, but we may summarise some of its features as follows. Jehovah is supreme over all the world. He does not force the nations to His will, nor is He the cause of their warfare. But he uses the changes in their conditions for His own purpose. His chosen nation must be ready to help in working out this purpose, which includes bringing the whole world to His feet in worship and offering. But to be Jehovah's chosen means a grave responsibility. If He puts Israel first among the nations, Israel must put

Him first in their lives. To neglect the localised centre of His worship is a grievous sin, and has to be punished as such. Since punishments and rewards must be looked for in this life, the failure of their harvests is a sure sign of His displeasure, although they had failed to see this. Their suffering is a result of their sin. But their adversity is God's opportunity, and must be seized by His prophet, who speaks in His name. And he feels justified in promising that a change to right action is certain of reward ; blessing must come, and come forthwith, to those who have started to build the temple. It is easier to incur God's displeasure through the pollution of sin, than to infect the nation with a new holiness. But the latter can still be done. Nor must men sit still and watch what Jehovah works for their benefit. The shadowy promise of a Davidic king to inaugurate the new reign of peace still stands. And who is more likely to fulfil it than the man who is already in the position of their leader?

§ 4. His Style and Language.

His style has been regarded as feeble, and his language prosaic. This cannot be denied, but three things must be remembered. (1) He went straight to the point, and his bluntness and brevity were justified and rewarded by his success. (2) There are one or two passages which rise above the level of prose, such as ii. 6-9 and 21-23. (3) It is not at all certain that we have more than a summary of what he said. A compiler (who lived near enough to his time to have a record of exact dates) has edited what is probably only just enough of his prophecies to shew how it was that he was instrumental in having the temple rebuilt. The diction of the book must be judged accordingly.

§ 5. THE RELATION OF THE BOOK TO
THAT OF EZRA.

The general situation between 537 and 520 has already been discussed (see pp. x f.). It remains to point out certain difficulties arising from apparent contradictions between the narrative of Ezra iii.–vi. and the statements of Haggai.

(1) The former shews that the first act of the returned exiles in 536 was to set up the altar, and then 'the builders laid the foundation of the temple of the LORD' (iii. 10). But Haggai (ii. 18) fixes a day in 520 when the temple was 'founded.' It is quite reasonable to suppose that after the lapse of sixteen years a fresh beginning would again be considered necessary. But there is no need to think that Haggai refers to the placing of a single foundation stone; he is concerned with the date when the temple was 'founded' or 'begun,' and the setting of 'a stone upon a stone.' It is quite unnecessary to force Haggai's language into agreement by making it refer to the foundation in 536. See note on ii. 18.

(2) The book of Ezra gives entirely different reasons for the delay of the work before 520. The causes assigned are external, and centre in the opposition of their neighbours, who obtain a Persian decree by which the work is stopped (Ezr. iv. 1–5). Haggai, on the contrary, shews the fault to lie with the people themselves. They have built their own houses instead of God's, and instead of recognising His displeasure in the bad harvests which ensue, they make them the excuse for further delay. This difficulty vanishes when we remember that the prophet spoke direct to the people, intent on a single purpose with regard to them. But the narrative in Ezra was compiled two centuries afterwards, when it was only the external facts which mattered, and moreover it was natural to represent in the most favourable light the patriots of long

ago who had succeeded in the glorious work of rebuilding the temple.

(3) It is recorded in Ezra v. that, no sooner had the people responded to Haggai's appeal, than a further check followed through the interference of the Persian governor Tattenai, who sent a letter of complaint to Darius. Not a word is said about this by either Haggai or Zechariah. But it does not seem that the work was actually stopped, as it had been in 536, and the mention of Tattenai did not come within the prophets' message. Besides, it is quite probable that Haggai's prophecies were finished before the protest was made.

The fact that there is not absolute harmony between the accounts is really an indication that they come from independent sources, and are therefore much more valuable and trustworthy than more entirely uniform statements might have been.

§ 6. SUMMARY OF HAGGAI'S PROPHECIES.

I. The Prophecy on the first day of the sixth month of 520.

The message of remonstrance for delaying to build the temple.

The people have thought of their own houses first, and have brought the curse of drought upon them for so doing (i. 1–11).

[The result of the prophet's appeal. Encouraged by the promise of God's presence, they decide to begin work at once (i. 12–15).]

II. The Prophecy of the twenty-first day of the seventh month.

The message of encouragement in rebuilding the temple.

The restored temple will be even more glorious than Solomon's, and as a result of the present upheavals among the nations, the Gentile world will make their contribution to its glory (ii. 1–9).

III. The Prophecy to the people on the twenty-fourth day of the ninth month.

The message of hope, in removing the pollution incurred by their neglect. From that day the unfruitful seasons will end, and God's blessing is assured (ii. 10–19).

IV. The Prophecy to Zerubbabel on the same day.

The message of assurance, and the call to be God's representative.

The anarchy of the world will result in a Messianic kingdom, in which the leader of the Jews must take his part (ii. 20–23).

THE
BOOK OF HAGGAI

I. Haggai's Warning to the Jews of Jerusalem to begin without further delay the rebuilding of the Temple.

1–11. *The Prophet's Appeal.*

IN the second year of Darius the king, in the sixth **1** month, in the first day of the month, came the word of the LORD by Haggai the prophet unto Zerubbabel the son

---

i. 1. In the second year: i.e. 520 B.C. In the previous year the death of Cambyses resulted in a period of anarchy, during which Darius was the successful claimant to the throne. But Pseudo-Smerdis, who falsely claimed to be the brother of Cambyses, had first to be overthrown, and likewise other usurpers in different parts of the kingdom. However, the reign of Darius is dated from 521.

Darius the king. This is Darius I the son of Hystaspes, whose long reign lasted till 485. It was he who led the Persian expedition against Greece, which was defeated at the famous battle of Marathon in 490.

in the sixth month, etc.: a month of late summer. It began with a feast day, on which the people would be free to listen to the prophet's message.

by Haggai. The use of the third person shews this verse to be an introduction, by someone who subsequently collected the prophet's words into a book. This must have been before 424, as at that date Darius Nothus came to the throne, and it would have been necessary to distinguish Darius the son of Hystaspes from him, instead of simply calling him 'the king.' For the name Haggai see Introd. p. 1.

unto Zerubbabel, etc.: the civil head of the returned Jews, who had been made pekhah or governor of the Persian province into which Judah had been formed. His name occurs earlier, in Ezra ii. 2, iii. 2, etc., as the ruler of the returned exiles in 536, but it is uncertain whether he is to be identified with Sheshbazzar the prince of Judah (Ezr. i. 8) who actually led them back from

of Shealtiel, governor of Judah, and to Joshua the son of
2 Jehozadak, the high priest, saying, Thus speaketh the
LORD of hosts, saying, This people say, It is not the time

Babylon in 537. Zerubbabel's father Shealtiel (in 1 Chron. he is
his uncle, but see Matt. i 12) was the son of Jeconiah or Jehoiachin,
one of the last kings of Judah, who had been taken captive to
Babylon in 597. He was therefore of the royal Davidic line, and
likely both to be chosen as leader by Darius, and to be marked
out by Haggai and Zechariah as the centre of Messianic hopes
(see Hagg. ii. 23 and Zech. ii. 8).

and to Joshua: called in *Ezra* and *Nehemiah* Jeshua the son
of Jozadak. As Zerubbabel was of the royal line, so was Joshua
of the line of high-priests. His father had been carried captive to
Babylon (1 Chron. v.), where the son was probably born and
reared. Dr Barnes (*Cambridge Bible for Schools*, p. 2) notes the
difference in the life of the nation made by the exile. Before it,
a prophet would address his king only; now that the nation had
in some sense become a church, the spiritual ruler is naturally
associated with him.

2. Thus speaketh *Jehovah* **of hosts.** The prophet's first words
make it plain that he is acting simply as the spokesman of God's
own message. The expression **Jehovah of hosts** is a favourite one,
and occurs no less than thirteen times in this short book. It often
adds a solemn dignity to an otherwise bald style of diction, as in
the verses ii. 7–9, where it is repeated four times. At a time
when the clash of armies was being heard throughout the surrounding nations, it was a happy phrase in the mouth of the prophet
who was trying to make his countrymen realise that God was
using great world-events for His own purposes and the good of
His chosen people.

This people say, etc. The returned Jews had plenty of excuses
for not building the temple yet. It is true that this was the purpose for which the decree of Cyrus had allowed them to return
from their captivity in Babylon in 537 (Ezr. i. 3), and that on
reaching Jerusalem they had set up the altar of burnt-offering
amid the stones of the ruined temple. But there had been many
hindrances since then. The opposition of the alien population of
the neighbourhood had brought the work to a standstill for a
while. And a series of bad harvests had sorely taxed the resources
of the newly-returned community. No wonder that it seemed
better to make certain of houses for themselves first, and to wait
till fuller barns justified them in turning their attention to the
house of God.

It is not the time for us to come, etc. If this be the translation,
it means that they were too busy in the fields outside Jerusalem,

for us to come, the time for the LORD'S house to be built.
Then came the word of the LORD by Haggai the prophet, 3
saying, Is it a time for you yourselves to dwell in your 4
cieled houses, while this house lieth waste? Now therefore 5
thus saith the LORD of hosts: Consider your ways. Ye 6
have sown much, and bring in little; ye eat, but ye have
not enough; ye drink, but ye are not filled with drink; ye
clothe you, but there is none warm; and he that earneth

---

and did not yet want to *come* to the city and assemble for the
work. In the narrative which follows the prophecy, we are told
the result of the appeal thus, 'And they *came*' (i. 14). But the
R.V. marg. links the two clauses, following the Septuagint
version, and reading 'the time is not come for the LORD'S house'
etc.

4. Is it a time, etc. The prophet answers their excuse with a
stinging rebuke, purposely using the word 'time' in satirical
imitation of their plea. They thought they must settle their own
housing problem first, before starting on the house of God. But
the rebuilding of the latter was the object of their return from
Babylon, an obligation which they were ignoring.

in your cieled houses: i.e. your houses that are panelled, or
wainscotted. There is no reference to ceilings, the word is an
archaic one, and only refers to the walls. Not content with
having a roof over their heads, they were introducing costly
woodwork into their new houses. We hear of such things before
the exile, and Jeremiah speaks of a luxurious house as 'cieled
with cedar, and painted with vermilion' (xxii. 14), but this can
scarcely have been the case among so poverty-stricken a community as the returned exiles.

5. Consider your ways. The same expression is repeated in
v. 7, and the verb occurs in the solemn appeal of ii. 15 and 18.
The Heb. 'Set your heart on your ways' suggests the effort of
fixed attention. It is not quite clear what is meant by **your ways**.
Some would render it 'how ye have fared.' But it seems to refer
to the active side of their life, the actions which have been theirs,
and the results which those actions are bringing.

6. The scarcity caused by bad seasons is described according
to its various effects. The harvests have been no true return for
the seed expended; they have had food and drink enough to
support existence, but not to satisfy them; they have clothing
indeed of a kind, but not enough to protect them from the cold;
and wages go such a little way that they seem to disappear as
soon as they have been earned.

7 wages earneth wages *to put it* into a bag with holes. Thus
8 saith the LORD of hosts : Consider your ways. Go up to
the mountain, and bring wood, and build the house ; and
I will take pleasure in it, and I will be glorified, saith the
9 LORD. Ye looked for much, and, lo, it came to little ; and

---

he that earneth wages, etc. The earlier part of the verse
describes the husbandman's plight. The labourer is now shewn
to be no better off. The language is picturesque, and suggests
that the money goes as fast as if it were put into an old purse with
holes at the bottom through which it fell.

7. This repetition of the appeal suggests that they need to
realise that they had done even more than insult their God in
building their own houses before His. They had thought that
these bad seasons necessarily caused a further delay of their duty,
but really it was the delay that was causing the bad seasons. It was
God's punishment, as is plain from the verses which follow.
(Cf. also ii. 17, 'I smote you with blasting and with mildew.')
They must now consider what they can do to make amends.

8. Go up to the mountain. The prophet demands that heart-
searching shall at once result in action, and appeals to them to
begin building at once.

the mountain has been variously interpreted. It may mean
the hill on which the temple stood, which is often so called, as
in Isaiah ii. 2, 'the mountain of the LORD's house shall be
established.' But the R.V. marg. suggests another rendering,
which is in accord with the Septuagint, i.e. 'the hill country,'
meaning that they are to go off to tree-clad hills and cut down
trees for the building. It remains uncertain where this hill
country would be; Lebanon, which produced the cedar-wood for
the first temple, was too far away, and it is more likely to
be the hills of Judah or Ephraim which were once well wooded
(see Neh. viii. 15).

bring wood : for this had all been destroyed when Nebuchadrezzar's captain 'burnt the house of the LORD' on the fall
of Jerusalem in 586 (2 Kings xxv. 9). The stones would of
course be still lying around, so that new ones were not required.

I will take pleasure, etc. They may look for two results; God
will accept their effort, and He will also shew His glory (Heb.
glorify myself), either by blessing them or by receiving new
honour from them in the restored temple.

9. It is now made quite plain that the failure of their harvests
and the scarcity thus caused were due to God's anger at their
neglect.

when ye brought it home. Besides the smallness of the crop,
disaster befell that which was actually harvested.

when ye brought it home, I did blow upon it. Why? saith the LORD of hosts. Because of mine house that lieth waste, while ye run every man to his own house. Therefore for 10 your sake the heaven is stayed from dew, and the earth is stayed *from* her fruit. And I called for a drought upon the 11 land, and upon the mountains, and upon the corn, and upon the wine, and upon the oil, and upon that which the ground bringeth forth, and upon men, and upon cattle, and upon all the labour of the hands.

12–15. *The People's Response.*

Then Zerubbabel the son of Shealtiel, and Joshua the son 12 of Jehozadak, the high priest, with all the remnant of the

---

I did blow upon it. There are several explanations of this phrase. Mitchell (*Intern. Crit. Comm.* p. 48) takes it in the sense of breathing upon it, as bringing a curse, and refers to the Moslem superstition that to breathe on a threshing-floor full of grain could work magic and *spoil* it. Dr Barnes (*op. cit.* p. 7) favours the idea that when God is said to 'exhale' it is the opposite of His smelling or inhaling an offering, and it is thus a Hebrew idiom for *rejecting* it. The R.V. marg., in rendering 'blow it away,' simply suggests the idea of its rapid disappearance, like the wages in *v.* 6, and this is perhaps sufficient explanation.

run every man to his own house: i.e. concerned themselves with their own housing, others being included beside the richer members mentioned in *v.* 4.

10. for your sake: i.e. because of your wickedness. But the words are scarcely needed after *Therefore*, so perhaps it is best to follow the R.V. marg. and A.V. with 'over you.'

11. The meaning seems to be that the loss of the various crops, including the three staple ones of the time, made men suffer from it in every direction. But Dr Barnes takes the 'drought upon men' as referring to the scantiness of population among the returned exiles. But this is a little forced.

12–14. The compiler, who has already given us *v.* 1, here describes the result of Haggai's first prophecy. If we include in this section the last verse of the chapter, it appears that the work was begun on the 24th day of the same month, about three weeks after the prophet had spoken. But this makes it exceedingly difficult to explain why in ch. ii. *vv.* 10, 15, 18, the 24th day of the ninth month (just three months later) is of such great importance as forming the turning-point. That passage is greatly simplified by

people, obeyed the voice of the LORD their God, and the
words of Haggai the prophet, as the LORD their God had
13 sent him; and the people did fear before the LORD. Then
spake Haggai the LORD'S messenger in the LORD'S mes-

reckoning that date as the moment when they actually began to
build the temple. It is possible to reckon accordingly, if two
modifications are made:

(1) *v.* 14 must be treated (as in the Hebrew, which places a
full stop after it) as the end of the section.

(2) *v.* 15 must be treated as a separate statement, which is
incorrect, and the result of a confusion between the fact that the
first prophecy was in the 'sixth' month, and the fact that the
building began on 'the four and twentieth day' of *a* month, the
real month being the ninth, as in ii. 10, etc.

Such an explanation will affect the sense of *v.* 12. **Then...the
people obeyed** will mean that they listened to Haggai at once,
without waiting three weeks before acting on his advice. But
their preparatory work would take some time, and they could
not begin on the spot until three months later.

12. the remnant of the people: i.e. those who were left from
the nation which had gone into exile. The expression occurs
again in *v.* 14 and ii. 2. It may naturally be applied to the
returned exiles, but those who do not believe in such a return
take it as a proof that the population of Jerusalem now consisted
of those who were left behind by Nebuchadrezzar 'to be vine-
dressers and husbandmen' (2 Kings xxv. 12). Others take it
simply as 'the rest' of the people, in contrast with their two
leaders, under whose guidance they act.

the people did fear: since they had realised their neglect and
its relation to their present misfortunes.

13. the Lord's messenger. This expression is unusual for a
human messenger like the prophet, being generally applied to an
angel as Jehovah's messenger and representative. In Zechariah
i. and iii. such an angelic messenger appears frequently, and this
is the regular use of the word in the O.T. Three lines of interpretation have been suggested. (1) The verse is not part of the
book, but a gloss added in later times. (2) It is to be translated
'And Haggai said, The angel of Jehovah *is here* with a message
of Jehovah for the people.' This is in entire accord with the
language of his fellow-prophet Zechariah. (For the ideas underlying it, see note on Zech. i. 11, p. 41.) (3) The words can be
retained as referring to Haggai, the phrase being almost without
parallel, but not quite, for in Malachi i. 1 the word given as
'Malachi' simply means 'my messenger.' (In that passage it does
not matter whether the prophet's name is given or not; the fact

sage unto the people, saying, I am with you, saith the
LORD. And the LORD stirred up the spirit of Zerubbabel 14
the son of Shealtiel, governor of Judah, and the spirit of
Joshua the son of Jehozadak, the high priest, and the spirit
of all the remnant of the people; and they came and did
work in the house of the LORD of hosts, their God, in the 15
four and twentieth day of the month, in the sixth *month*,
in the second year of Darius the king.

II. HAGGAI'S FURTHER PROPHECIES OF ENCOURAGEMENT TO THE BUILDERS.

1–9. *The promise of future glory for the Temple.*

In the seventh *month*, in the one and twentieth *day* of **2**
the month, came the word of the LORD by Haggai the

---

remains that the word is applied to a human messenger.) This
last interpretation may therefore be allowed to stand.

I am with you. As soon as the people accept the prophet's
warning, they receive the encouragement that they sorely need,
for the work was full of difficulty. The words are repeated in
ii. 4, and have the same effect as the assurance given long before
by Isaiah in the word Immanuel, God with us. (Is. vii. 14 and
viii. 10.)

14. stirred up the spirit: the same phrase is used in Ezra i. 5
for the impulse which had led them to return to Jerusalem sixteen
years before in response to the decree of Cyrus ('whose spirit
God had stirred to go up to build the house of the LORD').

did work: i.e. performed service, the word for 'work' being
a noun. It need not mean that they actually began to rebuild,
but only that they set to work to clear the site and to make
preparations.

15. This date may be taken in three ways. (1) It gives the
actual date when they started the work. But this is difficult in
view of the later date given in ch. ii. See note on *vv.* 12-14
above, and Introd. p. 6. (2) It is an erroneous statement of date
made by the compiler, whose error the Hebrew text tries to cover
by inserting a full stop after *v.* 14. If this is the case, he has
combined 'the sixth month' of ch. i. with 'the four and
twentieth day' of ch. ii. (3) Stress must be laid on the fact that
this was only preliminary work, God's blessing being dated from
the time three months later when the actual rebuilding was begun.

ii. 1-9. The further their preparations went, the more they

2 prophet, saying, Speak now to Zerubbabel the son of
Shealtiel, governor of Judah, and to Joshua the son of
Jehozadak, the high priest, and to the remnant of the
3 people, saying, Who is left among you that saw this house
in its former glory? and how do ye see it now? is it not
4 in your eyes as nothing? Yet now be strong, O Zerubbabel,
saith the LORD; and be strong, O Joshua, son of Jehozadak,
the high priest; and be strong, all ye people of the land,
saith the LORD, and work: for I am with you, saith the

must have been impressed with the former beauty of the ruined
temple, and the impossibility of reproducing it. So, within two
months of his former warning, the prophet now gives them
encouragement in their resolve. Not only are they to feel the
presence of God now in their midst (i. 13 and ii. 4), but they
may be sure that the future holds blessing for the temple as well
as for themselves. Thus the prophet foretells the glory that is to
come.

1. the one and twentieth day. This was the seventh day of
the autumn festival, the feast of Tabernacles. This again (see
note on i. 1) would be a good day for the prophet to find the
people at leisure to listen to him. The harvest time was now
over, and its scantiness was realised afresh. With shame as well
as disappointment in their hearts, and an apparently hopeless task
in front of them, they needed something more than the festival to
encourage them.

2. to Zerubbabel, etc. See notes on i. 1 and ii. 23.

3. Who is left, etc. It was sixty-six years since the temple had
been burnt at the fall of Jerusalem in 586, so there can only have
been very few left in 520 who had seen it. But sixteen years
before this, when they first returned from Babylon, we are told,
in Ezra iii. 12, that there were '*many* of the priests and Levites
and heads of fathers' houses, the old men that had seen the first
house.'

This verse makes the theory untenable that 'Darius the king'
was Darius Nothus, who began to reign in 424 B.C., for then the
question would be useless, if not ridiculous.

this house. Enough of it must have been still standing to
make them feel that it was the same temple which they were
about to rebuild.

4. be strong: i.e. of good courage. It was thus that Moses
had encouraged Joshua (Josh. i. 6 and 9). Haggai depresses
them only to give them fresh encouragement by his threefold
exhortation, based on the assurance of God's presence (cf. i. 13).

LORD of hosts, *according to* the word that I covenanted 5
with you when ye came out of Egypt, and my spirit abode
among you: fear ye not. For thus saith the LORD of hosts: 6
Yet once, it is a little while, and I will shake the heavens,
and the earth, and the sea, and the dry land; and I will 7

---

5. according to the word, etc. In the Heb. there is nothing to
govern the accusative **word**. Various explanations have been given.

(1) The A.V. and R.V. insert **according to**, but without any
justification. (2) The R.V. marg. inserts a verb, as has to be
done in a similar passage in Zech. vii. 7, and renders 'Remember
the word.' (3) Many commentators follow the Septuagint in
omitting this clause as a later gloss. This gives excellent sense,
as *v.* 4 is appropriately continued by 'and my spirit abideth
among you.' (This is the reading of R.V. marg., instead of
abode.)

If a further suggestion may be hazarded, perhaps it is some
argument for the retention of the clause that it would be appropriate as uttered during the feast of Tabernacles. They had
just reminded themselves again of the Exodus and their time of
dwelling in booths in the wilderness. God had then fulfilled His
promise that His presence should be with them, and justified the
encouragement given to Joshua and the people (see note on *v.* 4
above).

6-9. This is the promise on which the previous words of encouragement are based. The prophet now rises from the matter-
of-fact level of his utterances hitherto, and declares what is the
mind of God in the future as well as the present. He sees a new
hope for his nation in the very disturbances by which the world
was being upheaved. He anticipated that the anarchy in the
Persian empire would lead to even greater disturbances, but that
the result would be that the whole world would take part in the
glorification of the restored temple, and that Jerusalem would
become the centre of peace and blessing.

Such an expectation had been echoed from one prophet to
another, and is reminiscent of that familiar promise, given both
in Isaiah ii. and Micah iv., that all nations should flow into 'the
mountain of the LORD's house.' When the time came that nation
should not lift up sword against nation, their mutual invitation
was to be 'Come ye, and let us go up...to the house of the God
of Jacob' (Is. ii. 3).

6. a little while. That the prophet expected an immediate
fulfilment of his words is shewn by the private prophecy to
Zerubbabel two months later (*vv.* 20-23) where his name is connected with the establishment of a Messianic kingdom.

I will shake the heavens, etc. The convulsions throughout

shake all nations, and the desirable things of all nations
shall come, and I will fill this house with glory, saith the

---

the Persian empire are pictured as spreading through the whole
universe. Haggai does not know that Darius has the situation in
hand, and will soon make things as before. He hopes for
stupendous changes which will leave his own nation supreme, as
v. 22 shews yet more plainly.

7. the desirable things of all nations shall come. This is
the most famous verse in the book, and one of the most disputed
with regard to its actual meaning.

(1) The A.V. follows the Latin rendering 'veniet desideratus
cunctis gentibus,' and gives 'the desire of all nations shall
come,' referring the words directly to the Messiah. His filling
the house with glory is regarded as fulfilled in the coming of
Christ into the temple, and this passage therefore forms the lesson
for the Feast of the Purification, or Presentation of Christ in the
temple. But the fact that the verb 'shall come' is a plural
makes this interpretation untenable.

(2) The R.V. keeps the plural and makes it neuter, viz. 'the
desirable things.' This must mean that the nations will bring
their treasures, their silver and their gold, and present them for
the service of the restored temple. This makes good sense, but it
anticipates the 'silver and gold' of the next verse, and also
omits the thought (expressed in the earlier prophets) that the
nations would come themselves.

(3) Others (see Dr Barnes, *op. cit.* p. 12) take the plural as mas-
culine, and refer it to the nations just mentioned. 'The desired
(ones) of all nations shall come' is explained as 'those of the
nations whom Jehovah desires shall come to worship in the new
temple.'

The passage may be regarded as Messianic in any case; the
only question is whether the personal Messiah is referred to or
not. Though we must make the reference less definite than was
formerly thought, it is thus brought into accord with the outlook
of the prophets. If the saviour of human society was personified
by them, they looked to someone of their own time, and
Zerubbabel was marked out as such by Haggai in *v.* 23, and
still more plainly by Zechariah (Zech. iii. 9, etc.).

I will fill this house with glory. The meaning of this will
depend partly on that of the previous sentence. If the 'desirable
things' are costly offerings, we may take the glory in the
material sense of a beautified temple. But if it is the nations
themselves that will enter, their worship will bring God the
greater glory. This is a more spiritual interpretation, and the only
thing against it is the phrase in *v.* 3, 'this house in its former
glory,' where the reference is plainly to material splendour.

LORD of hosts. The silver is mine, and the gold is mine, 8 saith the LORD of hosts. The latter glory of this house 9 shall be greater than the former, saith the LORD of hosts: and in this place will I give peace, saith the LORD of hosts.

10-19. *The end of the people's pollution, and the beginning of blessing on their land.*

In the four and twentieth *day* of the ninth *month*, in the 10 second year of Darius, came the word of the LORD by Haggai the prophet, saying, Thus saith the LORD of hosts: 11

---

8. God will only be claiming what is His own. This verse seems to follow most naturally if we take the previous one as referring to the treasures which the nations would bring.

9. Can Haggai have thought that in actual splendour this second temple would surpass the first? If so, his hope was far from justified. But in any case its glory is shewn to include the fact of its being the centre of peace. If 'glory' be given its more spiritual meaning, it will include the worship of the Gentiles, and may be said to point on to the glory of Christ's presence within it, and the coming of the kingdom of the Prince of Peace. (No allusion has been made to the connexion of this 'glory' with the Shekinah or visible presence of Jehovah in the holy of holies, this being no longer an accepted interpretation.)

10-19. This is Haggai's third prophecy, uttered after the lapse of another two months. But in the meantime his fellow-prophet Zechariah, fired, it may be, by his bold example, has echoed his appeal. In Zech. i. 2-6 is a brief but impressive call to repentance, giving God's message of 'Return unto me, and I will return unto you.'

10. the four and twentieth day of the ninth month. This is evidently the date of supreme importance, and in *vv.* 15 and 18 it marks the change in Jehovah's attitude towards His neglectful people. Hence the theory that it was on this day, and not three months earlier, as i. 15 would suggest, that the actual foundation was laid, and the rebuilding of the stonework begun. (See notes on i. 15 and ii. 15.)

11. Thus saith the Lord, etc. The people evidently are still in need of encouragement. As before, Haggai first explains their failure and then promises a change. Perhaps his words are in answer to objections on their part that no answer has yet come from God, and the words of Zechariah (i. 3) suggest that the bulk of the people had not yet given proof of inward change. It is to be noted that this time Haggai does not address their two leaders.

By an appeal to a familiar rule concerning ceremonial unclean-

12 Ask now the priests concerning the law, saying, If one
bear holy flesh in the skirt of his garment, and with his
skirt do touch bread, or pottage, or wine, or oil, or any
meat, shall it become holy? And the priests answered and
13 said, No. Then said Haggai, If one that is unclean by a
dead body touch any of these, shall it be unclean? And
14 the priests answered and said, It shall be unclean. Then
answered Haggai and said, So is this people, and so is
this nation before me, saith the LORD; and so is every
work of their hands; and that which they offer there is

---

ness, the prophet shews that until now they were all so polluted
by their neglect of God, that their offerings were useless. The
'deadness' of God's house was enough to cast a blight over
everything. But now that the reproach was removed, God would
accept them from that day.

12. Ask now the priests concerning the law. The prophet
himself is told to appeal to the persons whose duty it was to give
instruction in ceremonial regulations. He is to ask them, not
'concerning the law,' but 'for an oral direction,' which is the
original meaning of *torah*, the Hebrew for law.

holy flesh: i.e. part of the victim which had been offered in
sacrifice. In the case of the peace-offering, the sacrificer would
be allowed to carry some of it home. There is no doubt that the
effect of direct contact with holy flesh was enough to bring holiness, for it is laid down in Levit. vi. 27, 'Whatsoever shall touch
the flesh thereof shall be holy.' The question here is whether
such holiness can be transmitted to a third object.

13. unclean by a dead body. Not only the contact but even
the presence of a dead body was enough to cause ceremonial uncleanness (see Numb. xix. 14), which extended to anything the
unclean person touched. Thus pollution was far more easily
communicable than holiness.

14. So is this people. Their contact with their God, such as
it was, was not sufficient to sanctify the rest of their life and
work. On the contrary, the pollution which their neglect of God
and the deadness of His temple had caused, was sufficient to
spoil even the religious side of their life, as embodied in their
sacrifices.

every work of their hands. In the earlier prophets this would
mean their conduct and practices. But here it seems to refer to
their crops and cattle, which are the result of their agricultural
operations, for this is quite plainly the meaning in *v.* 17 (cf.
Deut. xxviii. 11, 12). Thus anything that they bring in as
offerings to God is already polluted, and can bring no blessing.

unclean. And now, I pray you, consider from this day and 15
upward, from before a stone was laid upon a stone in the
temple of the LORD: through all that time, when one came 16
to an heap of twenty *measures*, there were but ten; when
one came to the winefat for to draw out fifty vessels, there
were but twenty. I smote you with blasting and with 17
mildew and with hail in all the work of your hands; yet
ye *turned* not to me, saith the LORD. Consider, I pray 18

---

they offer there: i.e. on the altar which had been set up in 536
within the ruined temple. Driver (*Century Bible*, p. 164) calls
this 'a contemptuous reference to the provisional altar.'

15. consider: see note on i. 5, and notice that it is repeated
twice in *v.* 18.

from this day and upward. If **upward** is taken to mean
'backward,' then they are told to look back on the recent past
with all its failures and disappointments. The day was a turning
point, as marking the beginning of actual building. The trials of
the time before it are contrasted with the blessings which will
begin there and then. But Nowack (followed by Driver) questions
the sense of 'backward' for this word **upward**, and would make
it mean 'onwards.' In this case *v.* 19 must refer to the future,
and the first question must be followed by 'Do the vine etc. still
not bear?' the answer being that they will have begun to do so
with the new prosperity brought by the blessing. This somewhat
forced interpretation does not seem necessary.

16. an heap of twenty measures: i.e. a pile of unthreshed corn
which should in ordinary years have produced twenty.

winefat. This archaic form has been retained in the R.V. (cf.
Mark xii. 1), and means the vat in which the juice was collected
when the grapes were trodden in the winepress.

fifty vessels: properly fifty *purah*, which is the word translated
'winepress' in Is. v. 2.

17. with blasting and with mildew: i.e. with blight and
yellowness. The former was the result of the scorching east wind,
the latter was a blight which prevented the ears from producing
grain.

yet ye turned not to me: lit. 'Ye were not towards me.'
The phrase comes from the same verse of Amos as that which
suggested the earlier clause. 'I have smitten you with blasting
and mildew...yet have ye not returned unto me, saith the LORD'
(Amos iv. 9). Possibly Haggai consciously used the words of
the older prophet. But it has been suggested that the words
were not Haggai's, but were added later by one who had the
words of Amos in mind.

you, from this day and upward, from the four and
twentieth day of the ninth *month*, since the day that the
19 foundation of the LORD'S temple was laid, consider it. Is
the seed yet in the barn? yea, the vine, and the fig tree,
and the pomegranate, and the olive tree hath not brought
forth; from this day will I bless *you*.

> 20-23. *The promise to Zerubbabel that the present un-*
> *settlement of the nations will lead to his exaltation as*
> *God's representative.*

20   And the word of the LORD came the second time unto
Haggai in the four and twentieth *day* of the month, saying,

**18. since the day that the foundation of the Lord's temple was
laid**: or, better, 'the LORD'S temple was founded.' In Ezra iii. 10
we are told that in 536 the returned exiles 'laid the foundation
of the temple of the LORD.' Haggai's words seem to contradict
this statement. Some would take that occasion as the one to
which the prophet refers, bidding them look back sixteen
years. But this is scarcely likely, for there need not really be a
contradiction. For we may note (1) that, as the work was not
continued in 536, it may well have been thought right to lay the
foundation over again in 520, and (2) that Haggai does not here
speak of a foundation stone, but only of the temple as being
founded or begun. Although the foundation stone may have
been already laid, it was not until that day that 'a stone was laid
upon a stone' (*v.* 15).

19. In characteristic style, the prophet first paints the mis-
fortune of the present, the empty barns, in spite of the harvest
being some four months distant, and the failure of the fruit-trees,
which ought to have given a recent supply. Then, in one abrupt
clause comes the promise, which would be fulfilled by natural
means in the success of the rainy season, upon which they had
just entered. Another interpretation is that although the wished-
for crops have not yet been harvested, and the fruit-trees have
not yet had time to bear, they may already make certain of the
promise of a good harvest.

20-23. Although spoken on the same day, this prophecy is
quite distinct from the last. There it is only the people as a whole
who are addressed, and the message is wholly concerned with the
internal conditions of their own country. Here it is a private
message to Zerubbabel, whose name is no longer linked with that
of Joshua. And it is concerned, as was the case with the second

Speak to Zerubbabel, governor of Judah, saying, I will 21
shake the heavens and the earth : and I will overthrow the 22
throne of kingdoms, and I will destroy the strength of the
kingdoms of the nations ; and I will overthrow the chariots,
and those that ride in them ; and the horses and their
riders shall come down, every one by the sword of his
brother. In that day, saith the LORD of hosts, will I take 23
thee, O Zerubbabel, my servant, the son of Shealtiel, saith
the LORD, and will make thee as a signet: for I have
chosen thee, saith the LORD of hosts.

---

prophecy (in ii. 6–9), with the nations outside, and the effect of
the upheaval which was taking place in the Persian empire. This
will result in a complete overthrow of worldly might by the hand
of God, and a beginning of the Messianic kingdom, in which
Zerubbabel, as God's vicegerent on earth, will play the part of
Messiah.

22. The dire effect of the 'shaking' is more fully developed
than in *v*. 6.

every one by the sword of his brother. It will be neither
Jewish intervention nor Divine intervention by which the world's
might is broken, but by a process of mutual annihilation. The
idea occurs frequently throughout the O.T., e.g. Jud. vii. 20,
1 Sam. xiv. 22. But if ever it was likely to be fulfilled it was at
the present moment of anarchy and revolt.

23. saith the Lord of hosts. This refrain is a favourite one
with Haggai, but its repetition in his final words impresses upon
Zerubbabel the fact that it is as God's mouthpiece that he speaks.

my servant. In the second Isaiah the idea of a personal
Messiah had given way to a personification of the faithful among
God's people as 'the servant of the Lord' (e.g. Is. xlii. 1, etc.).
But now the earlier Messianic language is recalled, and Zerub-
babel himself is given the rôle of Messiah.

as a signet. This is the ring with which a minister of the
king might be entrusted. But, apart from the royal signet, a man's
own signet was a treasured possession, for it could be used for
the seal which represented him, and gave the equivalent of what we
should call his signature. (Cf. Jer. xxii. 24, 'Though Coniah
were the signet upon my right hand.') Thus the word suggests
two things : Zerubbabel should be both representative of God to
men, and also secure in the position thus assigned him. Both
these ideas are continued in the clause that is added, 'for I have
chosen thee.'

Thus the book, which began with direct public warnings, ends
with noblest private encouragement.

INTRODUCTION TO ZECHARIAH,
CHAPTERS I–VIII

§ I. THE PERSONALITY OF THE PROPHET.

The opening verse, which is an editorial introduction to what follows, states that they are the words of 'Zechariah the son of Berechiah, the son of Iddo.' The only other place where he is mentioned is in the books of Ezra and Nehemiah (which once formed one book). In Ezra v. 1 he is called 'the son of Iddo,' and the help which he and Haggai gave towards the rebuilding of the temple is described. In Neh. xii. 4 Iddo is mentioned as one of the priests who returned in 536, along with the high-priest Joshua. Later, in *v.* 16, Zechariah the son of Iddo is placed in the list of priests in the days of Joiakim, Joshua's son. Although certainty is impossible, we may probably infer that his father was either dead, or less distinguished than his grandfather Iddo. And if the latter was still alive, and among the returned exiles, while Zechariah himself is mentioned in the next generation of priests, it is likely that he was a young man when he began to prophesy in 520.

The fact that he was a priest is fully in keeping with the view of the high-priesthood expressed in his book. Haggai predicted the exaltation of Zerubbabel, the civil ruler. But Zechariah couples with him the spiritual leader Joshua, as marked out for honour in the new era (see iv. 14 and vi. 11). And in the vision which proclaims the removal of the pollution of sin from the nation, it is the high-priest who represents them and has a fair mitre set on his head. And if he were a young man, this would agree with his position in relation to Haggai, whose lead he followed in urging the new efforts of the year 520.

An apparent reference is made to him in Matth. xxiii. 35, where our Lord is represented as saying 'from the blood of righteous Abel unto the blood of Zechariah son of Berechiah, whom ye slew between the temple and the altar.' But this is undoubtedly an error, and the Zechariah referred to is the son of Jehoiada, who was thus put to death by Joash (2 Chron. xxiv. 20, 21). The error may have crept into the text later, but in any case there was a tradition in the early Christian Church that it was the prophet who was thus slain.

His language is far more picturesque than that of Haggai, but it does not rise much above rhythmical prose.

§ 2. THE EXTENT AND NATURE OF HIS PROPHETIC ACTIVITY.

It is only the contents of chs. i.–viii. that can be regarded as his prophecies. For the reasons, see Introd. to Zech. ix.–xiv. pp. 75 ff. It was the dire need of the returned exiles in Jerusalem in the year 520 which induced him to speak, two months after Haggai had begun to do so. For the circumstances, see General Introd. p. ix, and Introd. to Haggai, p. 2. His theme is the same, viz. the rebuilding of the temple, long neglected, and now an imperative duty, if they are to exchange God's displeasure for His presence and blessing.

But whereas Haggai is content to urge the paramount duty of building, Zechariah goes deeper, and makes an ethical appeal, of which his first brief prophecy (i. 2–6) gives the motto, 'Return unto me, saith the LORD of hosts, and I will return unto you.' Three months later, he narrates a series of visions, which, under varied figures, enforce the same lesson (i. 7–vi.). Finally, two years later, in 518, he warns and encourages his countrymen along the familiar lines of the 'former prophets,' urging them to a course of just and kindly dealing with their fellows as a condition

of future blessing (vii.–viii.).   In all this, his message takes
up that of Haggai where it left off, and leads them on from
the outward effort to rebuild God's house, to the inward
efforts of spiritual reconstruction which must go with it.
This last prophecy was spoken when the work was half
finished, as we know from Ezra vi. 15, 16 that the temple
was completed and dedicated in 516.

§ 3.   His Theology and Message.

His message is so much more spiritual than Haggai's
(as has just been stated), that the discussion of it is
naturally connected with his own religious convictions.

(a) *His conception of God.*   Like Haggai, he realises not
only that Jehovah is in a special sense the God of His chosen
people, but that He is also the 'Lord of Hosts' who controls
the universe, and is thus the Ruler of all nations. (The
Septuagint rendering of the title is 'Almighty,' or 'All
Ruler.')   He follows the earlier prophets, from Amos
onwards, in their insistence that God is a moral ruler, who
requires those who worship Him to manifest moral qualities
themselves.   It is not sufficient to keep a fast, or any other
outward form of ceremonial, unless the spirit as well as the
letter be observed (vii. 5, 6).

A God of justice and mercy demands that these things
should shew themselves in the lives and actions of His
people (vii. 9, 10, viii. 16, 17).   He punishes them for their
sins by sending adversity, but He is equally ready to reward
them with prosperity if they will learn their lesson and turn
to Him again (i. 3, viii. 14, 15).   They may attract the
heathen, by the blessing they receive, to come and claim
part of it for themselves (viii. 13, 22).

In contrast with earthly might, is the 'spirit' of Jehovah,
the divine energy which makes men do God's work, and
inspires the prophet to speak His words.   All the while,
the thought of the rebuilding of the temple is in the
prophet's mind, and it often comes to the surface.   But
God wants more of His people than simply a House for

His Presence to rest in. These conceptions of the Deity continually find their way into the message he gives.

(b) *The Ministry of Angels.* The presence of angels is one of the remarkable features of Zechariah's visions. Unlike the earlier prophets, he does not describe himself as coming into direct communication with Jehovah. In Isaiah's call (ch. vi.), it was Jehovah whom he saw 'high and lifted up,' and although angels were present, and one of them was sent to reassure him, it was 'the voice of the Lord' that he heard. Already in Ezekiel's visions angels were present, though he speaks of them as men. And in the long vision of the restored temple, which would be of special interest to Zechariah, one of them acts as guide and interpreter to the prophet (see Ezek. xl. 1–4, etc.). If God's holiness seemed to Ezekiel to have withdrawn Him from direct touch even with His prophets, this was felt yet more fully after the exile by Zechariah. The visions are explained by an interpreting angel who talks with him (i. 13–19, etc.); there is one who rides on one of the horses of the first vision (i. 8, 11); 'another angel' appears in the third vision (ii. 3), and in the fourth vision the direct representative of the Deity is called 'the angel of Jehovah' (iii. 1).

Besides these 'angels' there appears in the same vision 'the Satan,' an accusing angel, who opposes, not God, but men, and acts under the orders of Jehovah (see note on iii. 1). His functions are like those ascribed to him in Job i., ii., and we must be careful not to connect him with all the later ideas connected with him as 'the devil.'

(c) *Sin and its results.* Sin brings visible punishment with it, and must be repented of. Amendment of life is what God requires, and not merely the fulfilment of ritual rules. Like Haggai, Zechariah recognises a national taint which is due to the nation's sin and neglect. This sin may be viewed as a corporate whole. The high-priest is seen in vision clothed in filthy garments as the result of it, and when he exchanges them at God's bidding for 'rich apparel' and 'a fair mitre,' it is a sign that the people's iniquity is pardoned (iii. 3–5). 'Wickedness' takes the form of a woman, who is transported bodily from the country, and set down in the midst of their former oppressors (v. 8–11). But at the same time he goes further than Haggai in teaching the guilt of the individual, and the punishment which each must bear for his own sin. This was a far newer doctrine, which had been discussed by Ezekiel and propounded in the assertion which sounds so obvious to our own ears, 'The soul that sinneth, it shall die.' This individualist theory of sin is strikingly set forth by Zechariah in his vision of the flying roll, which finds out the houses of sinners and demolishes them (v. 3, 4). The purging out of sin leads to fresh efforts to co-operate with God, and this is the way that His blessings are won and His work is fulfilled.

(*d*) *Social righteousness.* Zechariah sets before his generation, as the great lesson which his nation failed to learn from the prophets before the exile, the need of just and true dealing, both in the courts and in daily life (viii. 16, 17). True religion extends to care for the father-·less and widows, and mercy is of greater value than sacrifice (vii. 8, 9).

(*e*) *The Messianic hope.* Haggai had already linked the name of Zerubbabel with the new kingdom of peace and prosperity which was to begin among them (Hagg. ii. 22, 23). But again Zechariah goes further, and applies to him the Messianic name already used by Isaiah (xi. 1) and Jeremiah (xxiii. 5 and xxxiii. 15). A 'Branch' or 'Shoot' of David's house was to herald the new era, and Zechariah now encourages Zerubbabel with the thought of the honour being his (iii. 8 and vi. 12). Of course there is no thought of Zerubbabel being 'Messiah' in the later sense of the word. We need not therefore be surprised if so little of the prophecy was fulfilled. Zerubbabel either did not get the opportunity or had not the ability to assume the position suggested to him, but the fact remains that both prophets

were right in proclaiming that a new era began in 520 for
the returned exiles under his leadership. It was an era of
purer religion and higher patriotism, in which God's holy
house became the centre of their nation and its unity, and
the spiritual authorities came to be accorded the first place
in its life.

(*f*) *His relation to the earlier prophets.* Zechariah has
been charged with being a mere imitator of those who
had gone before him, following their theology, and repeat-
ing parts of their message, often in language identical with
theirs. It is true that he was not called upon to say much
that was new. His chief function was to warn and to
encourage, and he wisely drew his warnings from the past,
where the lessons of the exile were set out for their admoni-
tion. But his visions are too original to justify the charge
that he merely copied others. And the complete success
which attended the joint efforts of Haggai and himself to
stir the people from their lethargy to practical and laborious
action, shews that they must have both been men of force
and individuality. It is part of his purpose to remind men of
the message of the former prophets. He repeats it in each
prophecy when he is not recording his own visions. In·
the first prophecy, the words of i. 6 are reminiscent of
Hosea, Isaiah, Jeremiah and Ezekiel. And in the third
prophecy of chs. vii.–viii., he seems to echo the message
of the same prophets (vii. 7–10, on which see notes), perhaps
adding to them that of Micah (vi. 8). It has been noted
that there is a soberness and moderation in his language,
which shews no effort to improve on former utterances,
even in such themes as the glory and happiness of the
coming era of peace.

§ 4. HIS VISIONS.

(*a*) *Their nature.* Zechariah was not the first prophet
to set forth his message in the form of visions. They occur
occasionally in Amos (vii.–ix.), Isaiah (vi.), and Jeremiah
(i. and xxiv.), but it is in Ezekiel that we first meet with

a large use of them. His vision of the restored temple extends to nine chapters (xl.–xlviii.). Zechariah's, on the contrary, are all of them word pictures drawn in briefest outline. He describes them as taking place 'in the night' (i. 8). He lifts up his eyes, and sees what the angel shews him, and after the first four visions, he falls into a deeper trance, from which the angel wakes him, 'as a man that is wakened out of his sleep' (iv. 1). He declares on the same day the whole series of eight visions (i. 7), but does not necessarily imply that they took place at the same time. The question arises, how far they are actual dreams, or whether they are not more than a literary device, whereby the prophet enforces his message in arresting form. They are certainly a most effective form of teaching, and may in some sense be compared to the parables of our Lord. Many views have been taken with regard to their origin, but it is perhaps sufficient to suggest here that, if the prophet, after delivering his first brief message of i. 1–6, had become lost in thought concerning the crisis at Jerusalem and the call to build the temple, such pictures may well have formed themselves in his brain.

(b) *Their order.* The visions shew a sequence of thought. The *first* and last are very similar, telling of horses of different colours which patrol for Jehovah and execute His will in the four quarters of the earth. The *second* vision shews how the power of the nations that threaten them is broken by the agents which Jehovah uses. The rest are purely national. The *third* points to Jehovah's presence in the restored city as a better defence than any walls. The *fourth* represents the people, in the person of their high-priest, receiving in symbolic form the forgiveness of their sins, while the *fifth* places the civil ruler beside him, and proclaims that the two are the channels of divine grace to pour the oil of grace into the lamp of the nation. Dr Barnes (*op. cit.* pp. 25 and 37) would place this vision before the fourth, but at least it is appropriate that the high-priest should be first connected with the removal of sin, and then with the conveying of grace, and not *vice versa*. The *sixth* and *seventh* are closely connected; the one shews the purging out of sinners from the land, and the other the banishment of sin in the abstract from the entire community. The *eighth* makes a natural close, as echoing the first and extending its significance. The visions are therefore in some sort of order, but the record of them is broken off more than once; by a lyric epilogue after the third vision (ii. 6–13); by a promise to Zerubbabel, wrongly inserted in the middle of the fifth vision (iv. 6^b–10^a); and by a historical epilogue when the visions are over, enforcing their teaching about Zerubbabel, Joshua and the temple (vi. 9–15).

(*c*) *Their interpretation.* The visions are generally understood as referring to contemporary events, either those of the year 520, or those immediately before or after. This interpretation, which is followed in the notes, may be briefly expressed as follows.

The first vision. Jehovah's Four Horsemen (i. 7–17).

These appear just outside Jerusalem, and report the result of their patrol of the earth. All is still among the nations, which leads the angel to appeal for a judgement in favour of the chosen people. This refers to the results of the series of rebellions which followed the death of the Persian king Cambyses. The Jews had first been encouraged by Haggai (ii. 6, 22) to expect that the anarchy would grow worse, and a new age for Jerusalem would result from it. But, now that Darius was making his throne secure, this was not the case. The vision assures the Jews that the era of God's blessing will come in spite of it.

The second vision. The Four Horns and the Four Craftsmen (i. 18–21).

Four horns, denoting hostile power, are broken by four 'smiths' who drive them away. The four horns are the traditional foes of Jerusalem, who are still a menace to the building of the temple. They are driven off, not by the sword, but by peaceful means. The craftsmen may be the actual temple-builders, or the spiritual forces which God uses as His agents.

The third vision. The Man with the Measuring Line (ii. 1–5).

The angel stays a young man who is about to measure the limits of the restored city, and tells him it must be without walls, both because its population will be so great, and because Jehovah Himself will be a wall of protection round about it. The young man seems to represent the energy of the builders, who must be satisfied when the temple is completed, and must certainly not put any other form of building before it, as some had selfishly done already (Hagg. i. 4). The object of their building is a religious one. The immediate prosperity of the city leads the prophet, before he narrates his next vision, to invite those still in Babylon to return to it.

The fourth vision. The acquittal of the High-Priest (iii.).

The Satan accuses Joshua, but he is acquitted, and clothed by the angel in clean garments, in token of the forgiveness of past sin. A promise follows of a Messianic era, connected with him who is called the 'Branch.'

The high-priest represents the people before God, and the changing of his robes symbolises the acceptance of their repentance, which will lead them to a time of spiritual and material blessing which they may connect with the name of Zerubbabel.

The fifth vision. The seven-branched Lampstand and the two Olive-trees (iv.).

This lampstand with seven lamps needs no oil, but itself supplies oil to two olive-trees which stand by. On these trees are seen two 'spikes,' probably laden with fruit, which represent 'the two sons of oil.' The lampstand represents Jehovah, supplying the oil of His grace to His people, who are seen as two trees in order to shew that He is in the midst of them. The two 'spikes' upon them are their civil and religious rulers, Zerubbabel and Joshua, who are the channels through which God's grace and blessing will come. A message to Zerubbabel is interpolated in the vision, because it gives the same teaching—'not by power, but by my spirit.' In it Zerubbabel is pictured as placing the final stone on the restored temple.

(N.B. An older interpretation makes the candlestick to be God's people, who are supplied with the oil of blessing by the two olive-trees or spikes—Zerubbabel and Joshua. See notes *ad loc.*)

The sixth vision. The Flying Roll (v. 1–4).

A huge open roll, inscribed with God's curses, flies through the land and finds out the houses of sinners, which it destroys. The obvious lesson is that the individual is responsible for his sin, which will surely find him out. The community needs purging from open sinners.

The seventh vision. The Woman in the Ephah (v. 5–11).

Wickedness, in the form of a woman, is thrust into a large measure or barrel, and carried bodily out of the land and deposited in Babylonia. The nation's sin is represented in the abstract, and the lesson is that it must be removed right out of the land. A vindictive touch is added in its being taken to its natural home, the land of the nation's traditional oppressors.

The eighth vision. The Four Chariots (vi. 1–8).

Like the horsemen in the first vision, these are sent forth from God through the earth to do His bidding. Those who go towards the north are reported as having satisfied His anger there. The chariots are God's spiritual agencies, which go forth for the protection of Judah, and the punishment of those who have oppressed her. The punishment falls specially on Babylon, as it had already at the hands of the Persian conquerors, and was falling at that very time as the result of a Babylonian revolt in the year 520.

An entirely different interpretation of the visions has been suggested by Van Hoonacker (*Les Douze Petits Prophètes*, pp. 579 f.). Instead of referring them to the present and future, he considers most of them to point back to the past. This certainly helps to explain the language used with regard to Babylon, which was no longer a dangerous foe. But it was not likely that these exiles would forget what they had suffered, and in the disturbances of the year 520 it seemed more likely that a position of power would come to their former oppressors than to themselves. The following is a brief summary of Van Hoonacker's explanations.

The first vision. Zechariah projects himself into the past, to the years of the exile before 538 when the earth was quiet and the Babylonian empire still unshaken. The angel's message points to the nearness of the fall of their oppressors and the liberation of the Jews.

The second vision. The horns are the oppressing power of the Babylonian empire, and the smiths represent its overthrow by Cyrus in 538.

The third vision. The measuring of the city is part of the preparation for receiving back the exiles. Jehovah returns to dwell in the midst of Zion.

The fourth vision. The interpolation in the fifth vision (which most commentators place after rather than before it), is to be read along with the fourth. The conditions for the restoration of the temple-worship are on the point of being realised. The high-priest has now had the iniquity removed, and the coping stone will soon crown the temple. All the conditions being fulfilled for the return of divine favour, the people will be loaded with blessings.

The fifth vision. Here the prophet, who has already reached the present moment in the previous vision, looks on into the future, and the divine provision for the maintenance of the blessings received by the community. The seven lamps represent the vigilance of Jehovah, or the agents He uses for His purpose. The two olive-trees, if they are not Joshua and Zerubbabel, are in a wider sense the two kinds of power, spiritual and temporal, through which the divine purpose is worked out.

The sixth vision. The first five visions form a series, and give a survey extending over some thirty years or so of the nation's history, and following its sequence. The last three form another series, which begins in the still more distant past. In the first brief prophecy of i. 1-6, a relation has been suggested between the prophet's hearers and their fathers. This is now developed in the visions, and a contrast is drawn between their destiny, happy through the events of the Restoration, and that of a previous generation. Thus the flying roll is a testimony to the divine curse which came upon the guilty nation *before* the exile to Babylon.

The seventh vision. Here the period of the exile is reached, and a symbolical picture given of the pain of expiation involved in it.

The eighth vision. This refers to the era of the Restoration with which their blessing began, and the punishment inflicted on the Babylonian empire.

The historical appendix in ch. vi., though not in itself a vision, gives a purely ideal picture, and echoes the fourth and fifth visions in representing the blessings of the restored community under the rule of their two chiefs. At the same time it reviews the contrast (in the second series of visions) between their treatment and that of their guilty fathers.

(*d*) *The message of the visions in relation to the world of to-day.*

In a brief introduction and commentary of this kind, there is not space to draw attention to the many practical lessons which the prophet's words still have for ourselves. The great war has given us a fresh appreciation of the abiding value of much that found expression in the prophets of the Old Testament, and this should not be forgotten in any study of their writings. Perhaps this is particularly the case when the lessons are in so striking a form as that of Zechariah's visions. The present writer ventures to refer the reader to a book of his own, as indicating possible lines of study in this direction: *A Prophet's Visions and the War* (Skeffington, 1917).

§ 5. SUMMARY OF ZECHARIAH'S PROPHECIES.

1. The first prophecy, in the eighth month of the year 520.

A Call to Repentance, as the condition of the return ot Jehovah's favour. A warning based on the obstinacy of their forefathers (i. 1–6).

2. The second prophecy, on the twenty-fourth day of the eleventh month.

A series of eight visions, dealing with the great questions of the day, and intended to encourage the people in the building of the temple (i. 7–vi.).

3. The third prophecy, two years later, on the fourth day of the ninth month of the year 518.

The moral demands of Jehovah, which are a condition of blessing, and are still to be found in the words of the former prophets (vii.). A decalogue of promises, telling of the happy days in store for the community, if the divine requirements are fulfilled (viii.).

THE
BOOK OF ZECHARIAH

I. The First Prophecy.

i. 1—6. *A Call to Repentance.*

1 In the eighth month, in the second year of Darius,
came the word of the Lord unto Zechariah the son of
2 Berechiah, the son of Iddo, the prophet, saying, The Lord
3 hath been sore displeased with your fathers. Therefore
say thou unto them, Thus saith the Lord of hosts :
Return unto me, saith the Lord of hosts, and I will re-
4 turn unto you, saith the Lord of hosts. Be ye not as
your fathers, unto whom the former prophets cried, saying,

---

i. 1. **In the eighth month**, etc. This was in the great year
520 B.C., two months after his fellow-prophet Haggai had already
made a successful appeal to the returned exiles to fulfil without
further delay the object of their return, and rebuild the ruined
temple. Haggai had specially addressed by name their civil ruler
Zerubbabel, and their spiritual head Joshua. As they had already
responded, Zechariah had no need to do the like.

in the second year. See note on Hagg. i. 1 and Gen. Introd.
p. x.

the son of Berechiah, etc. See Introd. to Zech. p. 25.

2–6. This brief call to repentance forms the first prophecy. If
the words of Zechariah were edited afterwards, like those of
Haggai, this probably gives only a summary of a large message.
The people are warned that if they want God's favour, they must
seek it by returning to Him. They ought to have learnt the lesson
of their forefathers before the exile, who did not listen to prophetic
warnings, and were punished accordingly.

It may be noted that, except for the phrase 'Consider your
ways' (Hagg. i. 5, 7) Haggai is content with the practical appeal
to start building the temple. Zechariah goes deeper, and deals
with the springs of action.

4. **the former prophets**: those who had warned Judah of ap-
proaching punishment, and had been ignored. Chief among them
is Jeremiah (see Jer. xxv. 5, xxvi. 6, etc.).

Thus saith the LORD of hosts, Return ye now from your evil ways, and from your evil doings: but they did not hear, nor hearken unto me, saith the LORD. Your fathers, 5 where are they? and the prophets, do they live for ever? But my words and my statutes, which I commanded my 6 servants the prophets, did they not overtake your fathers? and they turned and said, Like as the LORD of hosts thought to do unto us, according to our ways, and according to our doings, so hath he dealt with us.

II. THE SECOND PROPHECY.

A SERIES OF EIGHT VISIONS OF HOPE AND EN-
COURAGEMENT, TOGETHER WITH THEIR MEANINGS,
AND NARRATIVES RELATED TO THEM.

7–17. *The First Vision. The Four Horsemen.*

Upon the four and twentieth day of the eleventh month, 7 which is the month Shebat, in the second year of Darius,

---

5. This verse has been variously interpreted. The question **where are they?** comes with strange abruptness. The point is that although those who spoke and those who ignored them have now passed away, Jehovah's words stand fast for ever. He adds that when the exile came, those who had ignored the prophetic message admitted that their punishment proved the truth of God's word.

Driver suggests that the prophet is here meeting an objection. They reply to his first words by asking, What have former generations to do with our own? He answers, in effect, that history repeats itself.

6. and they turned: but it was only the punishment which had this effect, not the appeal. So in their case the turning came too late.

7–17. The first vision must be compared with the last. Here it is Jehovah's four horsemen, there His four chariots. But the thought is the same, His control of the four corners of the earth, and His care for His chosen people in all His dealings with the larger nations.

7. the four and twentieth day, etc. This is exactly two months after Haggai's last two prophecies. This point is important, for he had indicated that the anarchy in the Persian empire would grow worse, and lead to a world upheaval, in which Jerusalem and Zerubbabel would be exalted. Two months had

came the word of the LORD unto Zechariah the son of
8 Berechiah, the son of Iddo, the prophet, saying, I saw in the
night, and behold a man riding upon a red horse, and he
stood among the myrtle trees that were in the bottom ;
and behind him there were horses, red, sorrel, and white.
9 Then said I, O my lord, what are these? And the angel
that talked with me said unto me, I will shew thee what

---

passed, and no change had come. In fact news had probably
arrived that Darius had taken Babylon and was successfully
crushing all his rivals for the Persian throne. **Shebat** was about
February, and is one of the new names for the months which
the Jews brought back from Babylon.

8. I saw in the night. For the nature of these 'visions,' see
Introd. p. 30.

behold a man: i.e. an angel. He seems to be the same as 'the
angel of the LORD that stood among the myrtle trees.' These
angelic beings are a feature of these visions, but they are found
also in those of Ezekiel (e.g. in chs. viii. and ix.). See Introd. p. 28.

a red horse: i.e. bay. It is curious that the colours of the various
horses have no meaning in the explanation of the vision (as is the
case in Rev. vi. 2, etc.). But the visions are so brief that such
graphic touches are valuable. (It is difficult to see how the
colours can be explained as some think, as representing the parts
of the earth which each had been patrolling.)

the myrtle trees that were in the bottom. The myrtle is an
evergreen shrub which still grows in the glens around Jerusalem.
Jehovah's angel has not yet entered into the city, but he is close
by, and ready to do so when the temple is built. It has been
suggested that some particular spot is meant by 'the bottom,'
but it means no more than 'the deep place,' or valley. The
R.V. marg. gets from the Septuagint the rendering 'the shady
place.'

sorrel: i.e. chestnut, a red that 'shines.'

9. what are these? To the ordinary eye they would suggest
one of the patrols which were wont to career through the Persian
empire, and had probably been often seen in the neighbourhood
of Jerusalem.

the angel that talked with me. This is a special angel who
appears in five of the eight visions, and explains to the prophet
what he is looking at. The Greek and Latin versions interpret
this oft-repeated expression as 'the angel that spake within
me.' But in ii. 3 he is seen to have a separate and visible
personality.

these be. And the man that stood among the myrtle trees 10
answered and said, These are they whom the LORD hath
sent to walk to and fro through the earth. And they 11
answered the angel of the LORD that stood among the
myrtle trees, and said, We have walked to and fro through
the earth, and, behold, all the earth sitteth still, and is
at rest. Then the angel of the LORD answered and said, 12
O LORD of hosts, how long wilt thou not have mercy on
Jerusalem and on the cities of Judah, against which thou
hast had indignation these threescore and ten years? And 13
the LORD answered the angel that talked with me with
good words, *even* comfortable words.

---

10. The angelic rider on the first horse explains that they are
Jehovah's patrols, who have returned from the four quarters of
the earth, after a tour of inspection.

11. And they answered. The subject is the 'horses' of *v.* 8.
But probably the riders are meant, for if the first horse had
a rider, the others doubtless had likewise.

all the earth sitteth still, and is at rest. This news sounds
like a wholly satisfactory report. But for the Jews it was scarcely
that, for they had hoped to benefit by the increasing upheavals
of the nations (see note on *v.* 7 and on Hagg. ii. 20–23). So now
some further encouragement is needed in the face of this apparent
delay on God's part to uplift His people. This is given by the
angel in the 'comfortable words' of *vv.* 14–17.

12. It is now the prophet's own angel who speaks. It is
interesting to note how clearly he is distinguished from the God
whom he represents, for he intercedes with Jehovah, and receives
a comforting answer to pass on to the prophet.

how long wilt thou not have mercy: i.e. 'wilt thou refuse
to have compassion' by avenging them on the nations which have
ruined their national life.

threescore and ten years. It is not easy to find a period of
exactly 70 years which will fit in with the exile. Even in 520, so
long a period had not elapsed since the destruction of Jerusalem
in 586, while the earlier captivity of 597 is a little the other side
of the mark. But it was Jeremiah who had foretold that number
of years, which thus came to be the regular way of speaking of
the exile. If we want an exact period, it may date back from 536
to the year in which he spoke his plainest prophecy in ch. xxv.
concerning the time that 'these nations shall serve the king of
Babylon seventy years' (*v.* 11).

14 So the angel that talked with me said unto me, Cry thou, saying, Thus saith the LORD of hosts : I am jealous for
15 Jerusalem and for Zion with a great jealousy. And I am very sore displeased with the nations that are at ease : for I was but a little displeased, and they helped forward
16 the affliction. Therefore thus saith the LORD : I am returned to Jerusalem with mercies ; my house shall be built in it, saith the LORD of hosts, and a line shall be
17 stretched forth over Jerusalem. Cry yet again, saying, Thus saith the LORD of hosts : My cities through prosperity shall yet be spread abroad ; and the LORD shall yet comfort Zion, and shall yet choose Jerusalem.

---

14. for Jerusalem and for Zion : i.e. for the whole city and for the most sacred part of it. Zion is used at first of the hill on the S.E. on which David built his city at first (see I Kings viii. 1), but it is later extended to the hill further north on which the temple was built (see Ps. lxxviii. 69, 70). It came afterwards to mean the whole city.

15. the nations that are at ease : i.e. enjoying the fruits of their cruelty and their conquests.

they helped forward the affliction. First Assyria and then Babylon had been the instruments in God's hands for the punishment of His people. Both of them exceeded their commission, as is said of Assyria, 'the rod of mine anger' (see Is. x. 5–7), and of Babylon in Is. xl. 2, at whose hand Jerusalem had received 'double.' The fact that a change had not come under Persian rule has led some to surmise that the vision is only of time past. But the change was not yet great enough to reassure the Jews, who were expectant of a Messianic kingdom.

16. I am returned. Cf. *v.* 3.

my house shall be built. The promise of a restored temple was now present.

a line shall be stretched forth : i.e. a measuring line, with which to plan out the restoration of the city. Cf. the measuring line of the third vision (ii. 1, 2).

17. My cities through prosperity, etc. Prefer 'shall yet overflow with prosperity,' as R.V. marg. For the extension of restoration to the surrounding cities, cf. Neh. xi. 25, etc.

18–21. The Jews still have enemies on every side, who threaten to prevent the building of the temple. But these will be overthrown, either by an equal number of agencies raised up by God for the purpose, or by the resolute attitude of the craftsmen who

18-21. *The Second Vision. The Four Horns and the Four Craftsmen.*

And I lifted up mine eyes, and saw, and behold four 18 horns. And I said unto the angel that talked with me, 19 What be these ? And he answered me, These are the horns which have scattered Judah, Israel, and Jerusalem. And the LORD shewed me four smiths. Then said I, ²⁰₂₁ What come these to do? And he spake, saying, These are the horns which scattered Judah, so that no man did lift up his head : but these are come to fray them, to cast down the horns of the nations, which lifted up their horn against the land of Judah to scatter it.

---

are at work on the temple. In any case the danger will be overcome by peaceful and easy means.

18. four horns. Besides the greater nations, there were lesser enemies at each point of the compass. The horn is a symbol of strength in the O.T. and is often used of material might. As the horses of the first vision are put for those who rode on them, the horns may here represent the animals which possessed them.

19. which have scattered Judah, Israel, and Jerusalem. The neighbouring nations frequently assisted some greater conqueror in reducing the Jews. (See 2 Kings xxiv. 2.)

20. four smiths : or, as A.V. 'carpenters.' These may be (1) spiritual agencies for the overthrow of their enemies (see Driver, *op. cit.* p. 189, where he calls them 'iron-smiths,' and pictures the horns as made of iron), or (2) actual craftsmen, who, as they 'are *come* to fray them,' seem to include those of other nations. This accords with the promise after the eighth vision, that 'they that are far off shall come and build in the temple of the LORD,' whether Jews or Gentiles. See note on vi. 15.

21. to fray them : i.e. 'to frighten them away.' He is of course thinking, not of the horns, but the heathen powers which they represent. The Persian empire had already checked the threats, not only of Babylon, which was now finally overthrown, but also of the tribes which were trying to stop the rebuilding of the temple. Can there be any reference to the decree of Darius, in response to the complaints of the local authorities, sending money and material to help in restoring the temple? (See Ezr. vi. 8.)

ii. 1-5. *The Third Vision. The Man with the Measuring Line.*

2 And I lifted up mine eyes, and saw, and behold a man
2 with a measuring line in his hand. Then said I, Whither
goest thou? And he said unto me, To measure Jerusalem,
to see what is the breadth thereof, and what is the length
3 thereof. And, behold, the angel that talked with me went
4 forth, and another angel went out to meet him, and said

---

ii. 1-5. The second vision has shewn that the blessing upon
Jerusalem will depend, not on warfare, but on the work of the
builders. But they are not to think of their new security as
depending upon walls such as men build. Jehovah Himself will be
their wall of defence. Nor is the city to be confined within certain narrow limits; the absence of walls will allow it to spread,
and yet be secure.

This is learnt by the prophet through seeing a young man who
is about to map out limits of the restored city with a measuring
line, but is stayed by an angel, with the assurance that the new
Jerusalem will be both too populous and too spiritual for such
limitation.

It is also to be noted that, in a more practical sense, this is the
policy which was followed by Zerubbabel, who may have followed
literally the prophet's bidding. No attempt seems to have been
made to build the city walls, until the coming of Nehemiah many
years afterwards. When it was done, it caused so much opposition
from their neighbours that in the earlier days, while they were
still so weak, it was perhaps the better policy to leave it undone.
They thus avoided the provocation caused by turning the city
into a fortress.

1. a man with a measuring line. This 'young man' (*v.* 4)
represents the energies and forward policy of the more zealous of
the temple-builders. But another view suggests that he represents
the party condemned by Haggai (i. 2-6) as caring for the city
rather than the temple.

2. To measure Jerusalem. The measurements would be those
of the city as it had once been. Nehemiah, before starting to
rebuild the walls, made a tour of inspection (Neh. i. 13 ff.).

3. went forth: either from beside the prophet, or (following
the rendering which represents the angel as talking *within* him),
from his hidden place within his mind. Dr Barnes explains it as
'became visible.'

another angel. This is not the angel among the myrtle trees
of i. 11, but a third angel, who plays a subordinate part as the
other's messenger.

unto him, Run, speak to this young man, saying, Jerusalem shall be inhabited as villages without walls, by
reason of the multitude of men and cattle therein. For I, 5
saith the LORD, will be unto her a wall of fire round about,
and I will be the glory in the midst of her.

6–13. *An Appeal to the Exiles to return in expectation of National Blessing.*

Ho, ho, flee from the land of the north, saith the LORD: 6
for I have spread you abroad as the four winds of the
heaven, saith the LORD. Ho Zion, escape, thou that 7
dwellest with the daughter of Babylon. For thus saith 8
the LORD of hosts: After glory hath he sent me unto the

---

4. as villages without walls. The prophets had already spoken
of these as places of quiet and freedom, e.g. Ezek. xxxviii. 11,
'The land of unwalled villages...them that are at rest, that dwell
safely, all of them dwelling without walls, and having neither
bars nor gates.' But here the thought is of a growing population
which cannot be confined within walls, a glorious promise to the
scanty numbers now within the city (cf. viii. 5).

5. It is the presence of Jehovah that will bring true protection
and splendour to the restored temple and city, cf. Hagg. ii. 7.

6-9. These verses are not now considered to form part of the
last vision. It is the prophet and no longer the angel who speaks,
and he addresses, not the returned exiles, but those who are still
in Babylon. His invitation to them is based on the three visions
of reassurance to Jerusalem which have preceded, and leads (in
vv. 10-13) to a fresh assurance of blessing on the holy city.

The passage must be regarded as a lyric epilogue to them.

6. flee from the land of the north. This is explained in the
following verse as 'Babylon.' Although Babylon lay due east,
the caravan route went northward. Also the idea of captivity had
always been associated with the north, ever since the ten tribes
were taken northward by the Assyrians. In the eighth vision it
is God's messengers 'toward the north country' that punish Babylon (vi. 8). But probably there were many who were transplanted
no further than Syria, and indeed the 'dispersion' was in some
sense **as the four winds of the heaven.** (Cf. Is. xi. 11.)

7. Ho Zion. Though still in exile, they are called by the name
of their beloved metropolis.

8. After glory hath he sent me. These words cause consider-
able difficulty. (1) As they stand in both A.V. and R.V., they
are a statement by the prophet (before he begins to quote
Jehovah's words), that, with a view to the latter's glory (or, to

nations which spoiled you : for he that toucheth you
9 toucheth the apple of his eye. For, behold, I will shake
mine hand over them, and they shall be a spoil to those
that served them : and ye shall know that the LORD of
10 hosts hath sent me.   Sing and rejoice, O daughter of
Zion : for, lo, I come, and I will dwell in the midst of thee,
11 saith the LORD. And many nations shall join themselves
to the LORD in that day, and shall be my people : and I
will dwell in the midst of thee, and thou shalt know that
12 the LORD of hosts hath sent me unto thee. And the LORD
shall inherit Judah as his portion in the holy land, and

---

win glory or success in his mission), he is sent to warn their oppressors that God's people are too sacred to be harmed. (2) But
there is a stop after 'glory,' which is recognised by R.V. marg.
We may then take it as an explanation—'After glory!' Dr Barnes
(*op. cit.* p. 35) suggests 'Follow my glory!' as a paraphrase, and
says it 'is to be understood as a motto (or war-cry) given by
Jehovah to His people to hearten them for the great enterprise to
which He calls them.' The rest of the sentence he apparently takes
as A.V. and R.V. (3) Others, including G. A. Smith, regard the
whole clause 'After glory hath he sent me' as a parenthetical re-
mark by the prophet (or possibly a gloss). The main sentence
will then be 'thus saith the LORD of hosts unto (*or* concerning)
the nations that spoil you (for he … eye), that, behold I will swing
my hand over them,' etc. (4) Mitchell (*op. cit.* p. 141) gives another interpretation of **after glory**, i.e. after the glory or splendour
revealed in the above three visions his next duty is as follows.

toucheth the apple of his eye: i.e. harms the thing he most
carefully guards as precious to himself. This seems better than
'harms his own eye (i.e. the oppressor's) by doing so.'

9. they shall be a spoil: i.e. the biter shall be bitten, but
through God's power, not that of the Jews.

10–13. The appeal changes into a fresh promise of future
blessing upon Jerusalem.

10. Jehovah's words are now addressed to Jerusalem: the restored temple will be the guarantee of the return of His presence.

11. many nations shall join themselves, etc. Haggai (ii. 7)
had already faintly echoed the older prophetic expectation that
the heathen nations should come and claim a share in this new
centralised worship. Zechariah ends his last prophecy with a
picturesque assertion of this hope (viii. 22, 23).

hath sent me unto thee. The prophet suddenly addresses
them in his own person, as in *v.* 8ª.

shall yet choose Jerusalem. Be silent, all flesh, before 13
the LORD: for he is waked up out of his holy habitation.

iii. 1-10. *The Fourth Vision. The High-Priest, his*
Accusation, Acquittal, and Assurance.

And he shewed me Joshua the high priest standing **3**
before the angel of the LORD, and Satan standing at his
right hand to be his adversary. And the LORD said unto 2
Satan, The LORD rebuke thee, O Satan ; yea, the LORD
that hath chosen Jerusalem rebuke thee : is not this a

---

13. The verse is reminiscent of Habakkuk ii. 20, ' The LORD
is in his holy temple,' etc. But here the promise is that He will
come from His heavenly abode to His earthly temple, after a
period (when 'all the earth sitteth still and is at rest,' i. 11) during
which He seemed to be asleep.

iii. 1-10. The vision consists of three parts. (i) Joshua is
accused by the Satan (1). (ii) He is acquitted and honoured by
Jehovah's angel (2-5). (iii) He is assured of access to Jehovah, if he
keeps His charge, by giving Messianic honour to Zerubbabel as the
Branch (6-10). The object of the vision seems to be to shew that,
although the guilt of their neglect of God's house has polluted
even the most sacred part of their nation's life, this is now being
removed, and God's blessing is leading them to a share in the
Messianic kingdom which is about to come.

1. Joshua. See Introd. to Haggai, p. 3, and p. 10.

standing before : i.e. as before a judge. It is not clear where
the scene of the trial is, for, as Joshua is present, it can scarcely
be in the court of heaven.

Satan: i.e. the Satan or Opposer, an angel whose duty it was
to bring forward the sins of man, though not to tempt him to
them. Care must be taken not to read N.T. ideas into the word.
See Introd. p. 28.

2. the Lord said. In *v.* 1 it was His angel. Two courses are
open, either to say that in *v.* 1 Jehovah Himself was really intended,
or that in *v.* 2 it must mean Jehovah's angel, it being possible that
part of the phrase has dropped out. In spite of what Dr Barnes
says (p. 40), the second seems the better explanation, for (1) it is
with the angels only that the prophet comes in contact in the
other visions, and (2) the speaker's words in *v.* 2 'The LORD
rebuke thee' seem to imply that it is not 'the LORD' speaking.

The opposer is severely reproved, for two reasons, (1) Jehovah
has chosen Jerusalem, and therefore will not punish for ever,

3 brand plucked out of the fire? Now Joshua was clothed
4 with filthy garments, and stood before the angel. And he
answered and spake unto those that stood before him,
saying, Take the filthy garments from off him. And unto
him he said, Behold, I have caused thine iniquity to pass
5 from thee, and I will clothe thee with rich apparel. And
I said, Let them set a fair mitre upon his head. So they
set a fair mitre upon his head, and clothed him with gar-
6 ments; and the angel of the LORD stood by. And the angel
7 of the LORD protested unto Joshua, saying, Thus saith the
LORD of hosts : If thou wilt walk in my ways, and if thou
wilt keep my charge, then thou also shalt judge my house,
and shalt also keep my courts, and I will give thee a place

---

(2) short of actual destruction, enough suffering has already been
endured.

a brand, etc. The expression is an echo of Amos iv. 11, and
suggests something badly burnt, and only just snatched away in
time to be saved from destruction.

3. filthy garments. The sight of a high-priest with dirty robe
and mitre was a painful one, and shewed how far the pollution
of the nation had reached.

4. those that stood before him: i.e. before the angel rather
than before Joshua; the subordinate angels seem intended, though
possibly it may be the high-priest's attendants, as in *v.* 8.

5. And I said. The prophet seems to have been unable to
contain himself at this pollution of the national priesthood, and to
have interceded on Joshua's behalf. But some of the versions,
followed by R.V. marg., read 'he said.'

a fair mitre: i.e. a clean turban. The word is not one peculiar
to the sacerdotal office, as is the case with 'mitre.'

with garments: i.e. with goodly official robes, the 'rich
apparel' of *v.* 4.

6. The solemn charge is of a personal kind, unlike the sym-
bolism of the previous verses.

7. wilt keep my charge. The charge may simply be that of
faithfulness. But in view of the mention of the Branch, it is
probably the charge to honour the head of the new Messianic
kingdom.

a place of access, etc. Joshua is promised something more
than the abiding exercise of high-priestly privileges. He is to
have free access to Jehovah Himself. **these that stand by** can

of access among these that stand by. Hear now, O Joshua 8
the high priest, thou and thy fellows that sit before thee ;
for they are men which are a sign : for, behold, I will.
bring forth my servant the Branch. For behold, the stone 9
that I have set before Joshua ; upon one stone are seven

---

only mean the attendant angels in the vision, already referred to
in *v.* 4 as 'those that stood before him.' The words have been
taken as promising a future life in heaven, but this is not part of
the theology of Zechariah or his age.

8. thy fellows that sit before thee : i.e. his fellow-priests who
are in the habit of sitting before him to receive his instructions.
Cf. Ezek. xx. 1, 'Certain of the elders of Israel came to inquire
of the LORD, and sat before me.' It is therefore unnecessary to
picture the other priests as forming part of the vision, and being
present then in the heavenly court.

men which are a sign: or 'men of omen that I am bringing
forth,' etc. Either their names are, like Joshua's own, suggestive
of blessing ; or their number may have been seven, and thus connected with the stone of *v.* 9 and the Branch to which it may
refer. Dr Barnes (*op. cit.* p. 42) says they are the men of the
deputation from Babylon who are spoken of in vi. 10 and 14 as
having come to Joshua. That is the other passage where the
Branch is mentioned, and they would be 'men of omen' as giving
promise that more would follow, in response to the invitation of
ii. 6-9.

I will bring forth my servant the Branch. The verse is
Messianic and must be compared with vi. 12, where 'the man
whose name is the Branch' was to build the temple and rule upon
his throne. The reference is obviously to Zerubbabel, to whom
the whole building of the temple is ascribed in iv. 9. It is not
merely a reference to the future, for the verb is rather 'I *am*
bringing.' **Servant** is reminiscent of earlier Messianic language.
Branch is not a good translation ; 'shoot' of R.V. marg. is better,
for it is the growth that sprouts from the ground, appearing
straight from the soil, and not the offshoot of a trunk. The word
had already become Messianic in Isaiah xi. 1, where it is said of
David's stock 'a shoot shall grow out of his roots.' The idea is
developed by Jeremiah (see xxiii. 5 and xxxiii. 15) where Jehovah
promises 'I will raise up to David a righteous shoot, and he shall
reign as king and prosper.' Here the word has become personal,
a title for the Messianic king.

9. upon one stone are seven eyes. There is much difference
of opinion as to the meaning of the stone set before Joshua. Is

eyes: behold, I will engrave the graving thereof, saith the
LORD of hosts, and I will remove the iniquity of that
10 land in one day. In that day, saith the LORD of hosts,
shall ye call every man his neighbour under the vine and
under the fig tree.

---

it a stone used in building the temple, or is it a precious stone?
And in what sense is the word 'eyes' used?

(1) As the temple-building Zerubbabel has just been mentioned, it may be the headstone which in iv. 7 he is destined to
put in its place. Joshua already sees it in vision, and the
seven eyes are metaphorical, symbolising the all-seeing providence of Jehovah, which is again referred to in the next vision
(iv. 10) as 'these seven, which are the eyes of the LORD;
they run to and fro through the whole earth.' **The graving
thereof** suggests some divine symbol, possibly being in the actual
form of eyes. Thus the central thought is of the completion of
the temple.

(2) The 'eye' of a stone is its gleam, and if a stone has seven
gleams it must have seven facets. This can only be said of a
precious stone. What is the object of such a stone? Some interpret it as an ornament for Zerubbabel (cf. the use of the crowns
in vi. 11), and the 'graving thereof' would probably be his name.
But then there seems no connexion with the rest of the sentence
'and I will remove the iniquity of that land in one day.' Others
regard the precious stone as an ornament for Joshua himself.
The high-priest's breastplate is said in Exod. xxviii. 21 to have
twelve jewels in it, each one 'graven' with the name of a tribe.
The same chapter (*vv.* 36–38) orders a graven plate of gold on his
forehead, 'that Aaron may bear the iniquity of the holy things.'
Even if we may not connect this reference to 'iniquity' with its
use in this verse of Zechariah, the removal of the ephod in all its
splendour was a fitting guarantee that the pollution of the community and its priesthood was now purged away.

10. God's favour will then be shewn by the prosperity of every
citizen. The image is a familiar one for peace and security,
and it had already been used in Micah iv. 4 in a Messianic connexion.

9b–10. These words, so difficult to explain in this context,
would come quite naturally after v. 11, where wickedness is personified and removed to Babylon. It is therefore considered
probable that that was their original position. For the reasons
for making that and several other changes in the order of chs.
iii.–vi., see the following note on ch. iv.

iv. 1–6ᵃ. *The Fifth Vision. The Seven-Branched
Candlestick and the Two Olive Branches.*

And the angel that talked with me came again, and **4**
waked me, as a man that is wakened out of his sleep.
And he said unto me, What seest thou? And I said, I **2**
have seen, and behold, a candlestick all of gold, with its
bowl upon the top of it, and its seven lamps thereon ;

---

iv. This is a convenient place to deal with the critical questions which have been raised with regard to the order of chs.
iii.–vi., for it is suggested that we should place ch. iv. before
ch. iii. If it seems too bold to make alterations in the undoubted
order of the Hebrew text, it must be remembered that it would
only be afterwards that Zechariah's visions were collected and
written down, when they might not have been given in the best
and original sequence. Besides such unconscious alterations in
the development of the prophet's message, there is one point in
which intentional changes may well be expected. The prophet's
object in more than one vision was to point to Zerubbabel as
Messianic king. To write down such passages quite plainly was
scarcely wise, for it might give offence to the Persian authorities
and arouse their suspicions. A study of the text reveals a strong
possibility that it has been wilfully obscured by the placing of
certain verses out of their context. Further, there are passages
where we are left in doubt whether the honour is for Zerubbabel,
or only for the high-priest Joshua. Here it may well be that the
personality of the prince and the praises of his leadership have
been concealed behind the less suspected spiritual leader.

The suggested rearrangement is as follows:

iv. 1–6ᵃ, followed immediately by 10ᵇ–14. (The two mentions
of Zerubbabel are thus linked in successive verses, and 10ᵇ answers
the question of iv. 4.) 6ᵇ–10ᵃ follow naturally after 14. If we
place the whole of ch. iv. before ch. iii. it will suit well as following on ch. ii., for both deal with Jehovah's presence. Moreover
the end of ch. iii. leads on to the opening words of ch. v. The
sequence will thus be: iv. 1–6ᵃ, 10ᵇ–14, 6ᵇ–10ᵃ, iii.

1. as a man that is wakened. He does not really awake, but
the effect of the preceding visions was to send him into what
might be called a trance within a trance. If iv. 1 follows immediately on ii. 13, the prophet's state followed on the bidding that
all flesh should be hushed, because Jehovah Himself was waked up.

2. a candlestick...and its seven lamps. Such a 'lampstand'
had stood in the tabernacle, and suggested the brightness of
Jehovah's presence. It branched out into seven lamps.

there are seven pipes to each of the lamps, which are
3 upon the top thereof: and two olive trees by it, one upon
the right side of the bowl, and the other upon the left side
4 thereof. And I answered and spake to the angel that
5 talked with me, saying, What are these, my lord? Then
the angel that talked with me answered and said unto me,
Knowest thou not what these be? And I said, No, my
6 lord. Then he answered and spake unto me, saying,

---

seven pipes to each of the lamps. This implies that there
were forty-nine in all, but the Septuagint and Vulgate suggest
only seven altogether, as is noted in R.V. marg. The Hebrew
may be rendered 'there are seven pipes (or spouts) and seven,'
suggesting that there are two things each connected with the
lampstand by means of seven pipes. These two things must
plainly be the two olive trees of *v.* 3

3. and two olive trees. The older interpreters all imagined
that these olive trees supplied the oil to the lampstand. But it is
better to take the opposite view, that they are themselves supplied
with their oil by the lampstand. If the lampstand standing in
the midst represents the power of Jehovah's presence, the olive
trees which it supernaturally supplies will be the people of the
Jews, who are thought of as only two in number so as to place
the divine Presence in the centre. That each gets a sevenfold
supply indicates the sufficiency of the strength supplied.

6ᵃ. After the words **Then he answered and spake unto me,
saying**, we must pass on to *vv.* 10ᵇ–14. Therefore for the continuation of this commentary see p. 54, and then return to the separate
prophecy which intervenes, contained in *vv* 6ᵇ–10ᵃ.

6ᵇ–10ᵃ. The verses 10ᵇ–14 should be read first, as the obvious
continuation of 6ᵃ. Otherwise the prophet's question of *v.* 4
'What are these?' is not only left unanswered, but the angel
talks about something quite different. But by taking *v.* 10ᵇ next,
we have the answer, 'These seven (i.e. the seven lamps of *v.* 2)
are the eyes of Jehovah.' It is uncertain where *vv.* 6ᵇ–10ᵃ are
to be placed. It is best not to remove them further than the end
of ch. iv., though Mitchell (*op. cit.* p. 190) would place them
after vi. 14.

6ᵇ. This is the word of *Jehovah* **unto Zerubbabel**. In this
new prophecy the head of the returned community is warned
that his activities must be devoted to completing the temple, in
reliance upon God. He must not be tempted to get together an
army, in order to take advantage of the civil wars which were
weakening the dominant Persian empire. A policy which sought

6ᵇ–10ᵃ. *Promise to Zerubbabel. As he began the temple,
    God will grant him to complete it.* (This promise is
    interpolated between two parts of the Fifth Vision.)

This is the word of the LORD unto Zerubbabel, saying,
Not by might, nor by power, but by my spirit, saith the
LORD of hosts. Who art thou, O great mountain? before 7
Zerubbabel *thou shalt become* a plain : and he shall bring
forth the head stone with shoutings of Grace, grace, unto
it. Moreover the word of the LORD came unto me, saying, 8
The hands of Zerubbabel have laid the foundation of this 9
house ; his hands shall also finish it ; and thou shalt know
that the LORD of hosts hath sent me unto you. For who 10
hath despised the day of small things? for they shall

---

success by joining forces with some other discontented nation or
party, was not the right one for God's people.

Not by might: the word may be concrete, as in R.V. marg.,
'not by an army.' This goes better with the abstract word **power**
which follows. With both there is contrasted the spiritual force
with which God will supply them.

7. O great mountain. The word is of course used not in a
literal sense, but for the obstacles which the returned exiles had
to surmount. The opposition of those outside and a party of those
within had already caused grievous delay in building the temple,
and doubtless other hindrances were still in the way. The prophet
in graphic language addresses the 'mountain' itself, and then
orders it to 'become a plain,' smoothed away by the efforts of
Zerubbabel.

he shall bring forth, etc. Thus is pictured the great day when
the temple is completed, and Zerubbabel puts the coping-stone
in its place, while the people applaud and cry 'Beautiful ! beautiful !' **Grace** probably means outward beauty, but some would
translate 'Favour unto it !' i.e. May all favour it ! a prayer for its
prosperity.

8–9. When Zerubbabel thus fulfils the prediction, all will know
that it was Jehovah who made the promise through the prophet's
lips.

9. have laid the foundation. As in Hagg. ii. 18 (see note) the
expression only means that he had founded or begun it, and does
not refer to a foundation stone.

thou shalt know. If this is right (as Septuagint), he speaks
directly to Zerubbabel. But prefer, as Heb., '*ye* shall know.'

10ᵃ. who hath despised, etc.: i.e. anyone who had despaired

rejoice, and shall see the plummet in the hand of
Zerubbabel,

10ᵇ–14. *Narrative of the Fifth Vision resumed. Explana-*
tion of the seven lamps and the two olive trees. An
added detail—the two olive spikes.

even these seven, *which are* the eyes of the LORD ; they
11 run to and fro through the whole earth. Then answered
I, and said unto him, What are these two olive trees upon
the right side of the candlestick and upon the left side

---

on seeing the first paltry efforts of the would-be builders, will join
in the hope and rejoicing on seeing the building as it rises day by
day under Zerubbabel's direction. (But the plummet is perhaps
used for the *final* testing when the top stone is put in place.) For
their natural inclination to doubt the success of their task, cf.
Hagg. ii. 3 and Ezr. iii. 12.

10ᵇ–14. For the sequence of 10ᵇ after 6ᵃ, see note on 6ᵇ–10ᵃ,
p. 52. The prophet now gets an answer to his question in *v.* 4
about the seven lamps. As the angel does not reply to his second
query about the two olive trees, he puts it again in *v.* 11. The
angel seems to have still remained silent, for if the olive trees
simply symbolised the Jews on either side of Jehovah (the spiritual
lampstand, supplying the oil), there was no significance in their
number. So the prophet, looking more closely at them, asks a
somewhat different question. What are the ' two olive branches'
or spikes, which he now sees upon the trees? The angel, surprised that he has not grasped their significance (*v.* 13), reveals
it to him, as being a matter of real importance. But he does so
in veiled language, though in 'the two sons of oil' Zechariah
could not fail to recognise Zerubbabel and Joshua.

10ᵇ. even these seven, which are the eyes of the Lord. In
the light of the fresh interpretation of this passage by modern
scholars, the verse had better run 'These seven are the eyes of
Jehovah, wandering through the whole earth.' See note on iii.
9 for a similar explanation of the stone with seven eyes. As the
lamps form part of the lampstand, so the eyes of Jehovah represent that aspect of Him which is His all-seeing and all-embracing
providence.

11. upon the right side, etc. The nation has God in its
midst. Older interpretations always took it for granted that the
olive trees supplied the lamps of the candlestick with oil. The
view here given is the reverse. It looked as though the energy
would be supplied by the Jews, and that by their own doing they

thereof? And I answered the second time, and said unto 12
him, What be these two olive branches, which are beside
the two golden spouts, that empty the golden *oil* out of
themselves? And he answered me and said, Knowest thou 13
not what these be? And I said, No, my lord. Then said 14
he, These are the two sons of oil, that stand by the Lord
of the whole earth.

---

were restoring the spiritual life of the nation by rebuilding God's
house. But really it was the oil of God's grace which flowed
through many channels and actually supplied the olive trees themselves with that which it was their function to produce. God's
grace was the true source of all their present energies.

12. these two olive branches. As the angel still gives no explanation, the prophet looks closer and sees a 'spike' protruding
from each olive tree, probably laden with an abundant supply of
fruit.

which are beside the two golden spouts, etc. This is a difficult description in many ways. The words are ambiguous in themselves. If taken as R.V., they may simply imply the position of
the two 'spikes' in relation to two spouts or pipes (the number
of which was given in *v.* 2 as seven, or forty-nine). But the R.V.
marg., following the A.V., makes the golden spouts the channel
whence oil flows from the olive spikes. This suggests that the
olive trees *do* supply the candlestick, in spite of what has been
stated above. The difficulty has been faced in two ways: (1) The
Hebrew text is regarded as corrupt, and therefore nothing can be
argued from the verse. Indeed, in the Hebrew there is no mention of oil at all, as the word for 'golden oil' is simply 'gold.' (It
may refer to the golden bowl of *v.* 2.) (2) The whole of *v.* 12 is
regarded as an interpolation, which stands wrongly between the
question of *v.* 11 about the 'two olive *trees*,' and the answer of
vv. 13-14. It may have been inserted in the text as an attempt
to explain Zechariah's obscure words, but gives an interpretation
of them contrary to the one he intended. But, if a new suggestion may be allowed, why should not the prophet be noting here
that the olive spikes supply oil, *not* for the lampstand, but for the
use of man? In this sense the two leaders, Zerubbabel and Joshua,
supply their fellows with the oil of strength and energy. But they
are themselves 'sons of oil,' supplied in their turn with these
things from the central lampstand, which is the grace of Jehovah
Himself.

14. the two sons of oil. This is a familiar Hebrew idiom (cf.
sons of Belial, thunder, etc.). The word for 'oil' suggests the
fresh juice, not as prepared for the lamp. It is not that they

v. 1–4. *The Sixth Vision. The Flying Roll, which is
God's judgment purging the land from sinners.*

5   Then again I lifted up mine eyes, and saw, and behold,
2 a flying roll. And he said unto me, What seest thou?

---

supply oil, but that they are full of it; not that they are mere
channels of grace to Israel, but that their source of supply is the
grace of Jehovah's spirit. The alternative explanation is given in
the A.V., 'the two anointed ones,' which might apply to the
means of outward commission given to the two rulers, civil and
spiritual. But the meaning probably lies deeper than that.

that stand by: i.e. as his servants. Cf. 'that stand by' in iii. 7
and see note.

Note on ch. iv.

It may be well to give briefly the old method of interpreting
the fifth vision. The lampstand is the restored Jewish Church,
shining with the light of the spirit. The oil is the supply of
divine grace, which flows into the lampstand from the two
spikes on the olive trees, whereby are represented Zerubbabel
and Joshua, the temporal and spiritual heads of the nation. The
teaching of the vision contains a message to Zerubbabel that it is
by the divine spirit, and not by earthly might, that the temple
will be completed, and the great day will arrive when he puts the
coping-stone in place. The day of small beginnings must not be
despised, and then the eyes of Jehovah's favour and blessing will
be upon their work. 'By my spirit, saith the LORD of hosts,' was
regarded as the key-note of the vision. If the olive trees are not
the two men, they may be agencies 'near to God and beyond our
ken' (Perowne, *The Cambridge Bible*, p. 88). This was considered to suit best with the reference in Rev. xi. 4 to the two
mysterious 'witnesses,' as 'the two olive trees…standing before
the God of the earth.' If the 'spikes' are not distinct from the
'trees,' it must be said that the prophet substitutes one word for
the other when he looks more closely at what he sees in the vision.

v. 1–4. This chapter consists of two kindred visions, both
dealing with the pollution of sin. But the first deals with the
concrete removal of wickedness, in the extermination of sinners
from the community. The second represents wickedness in the
abstract, in the act of being lifted up from the land, and carried off
to be a plague to their arch-enemy, Babylon. For the arrangement
of the visions according to sequence of thought, see Introd. p. 34.

1. a flying roll: i.e. a roll or book, of the kind on which men
wrote, flying through the air.

2. And he said: i.e. the interpreting angel, whom the prophet
has mentioned so often.

And I answered, I see a flying roll; the length thereof is
twenty cubits, and the breadth thereof ten cubits. Then 3
said he unto me, This is the curse that goeth forth over
the face of the whole land : for every one that stealeth shall
be purged out on the one side according to it; and every
one that sweareth shall be purged out on the other side
according to it. I will cause it to go forth, saith the LORD of 4
hosts, and it shall enter into the house of the thief, and
into the house of him that sweareth falsely by my name :
and it shall abide in the midst of his house, and shall
consume it with the timber thereof and the stones thereof.

---

the length thereof, etc. The roll was of enormous size, thirty
feet by fifty. It was unrolled so that the writing on it could be
read. The only thing to which we can compare this sight is an
aeroplane. As Jehovah sent it down (*v.* 4) it was evidently swoop-
ing down from the heavens.

3. This is the curse. The writing on the roll consisted of the
code of laws which was one of the chief features of their national
life. Many of the laws had penalties attached, and there are
passages in the written law, such as Deut. xxvii. 15 f., which
consist of a series of curses. The huge size of the roll suggests
the great number of the curses. The language recalls the vision
of a roll which appeared to Ezekiel, 'and there were written
therein lamentations, and mourning, and woe' (ii. 10).

every one that stealeth...every one that sweareth. The
punishment is not of course to be confined to these two particular
sins, but they are chosen out as types. For they are typical of the
sins then prevalent in Jerusalem, such as the prophet denounces
in viii. 17 as the things that Jehovah hates. 'Let none of you
imagine evil in your hearts against his neighbour; and love no
false oath.' They are also said to be typical of the two tables of
the covenant, for one is a breach of duty to neighbours and the
other of duty to God. (But if this were in the prophet's mind,
surely their order would have been reversed.) **that sweareth** of
course means 'sweareth falsely,' and very likely the words have
dropped out here which are added in *v.* 4, 'falsely by my name.'

shall be purged out. The word may also mean 'go unpunished.' The Heb. has therefore been emended by some so
as to give the sense 'For how long hath every one that stealeth
been unpunished,' etc. This implies that Jehovah has been too
lenient, and now resolves to act with a new strictness against sin.

4. it shall enter into the house, etc. Its very size would
make certain that it destroyed alike the stone-work and the wood-

5-11. *The Seventh Vision. The Woman in the Ephah,*
which is wickedness removed from the land.

5   Then the angel that talked with me went forth, and
said unto me, Lift up now thine eyes, and see what is
6 this that goeth forth. And I said, What is it? And he
said, This is the ephah that goeth forth. He said more-
7 over, This is their resemblance in all the land : (and behold, there was lifted up a talent of lead :) and this is a

---

work of the house. Nor was the 'crash' merely the impact of a
moment; it would 'abide' there, which Dr Barnes translates
'pass the night.' The destruction of a man's house or tent was a
familiar Jewish punishment, and symbolised his being cut off
from the community.

Possibly the 'timber' and 'stones' suggest that such a man is
among those denounced in Hagg. i. 4, as having selfishly elabo-
rated their houses. In any case he is enriched by his thefts and
false oaths.

Some see a further lesson in this vision, as suggested by *v.* 4.
The question had been largely discussed (e.g. in Ezekiel xviii.),
whether a community was involved in the sin of one of its individuals or not. It is here plainly declared that it is not, and
only 'the soul that sinneth, it shall die.'

5-11. This vision shews that not only will sinners be purged
out of the new community, but the living principle of wickedness
will be banished from their midst. The previous vision was a
warning, concerning the destruction of sinners; this one is an
encouragement, concerning the removal of sin. The vindictive
touch at the end (*vv.* 10-11) reveals the inborn hatred of the Jew
against Babylon.

5. went forth: or rather 'came forth,' either by becoming
visible (see note on ii. 3) or by again coming into view after the
darkness of the previous vision.

6. the ephah. This was a large measure of capacity, amount-
ing to some nine gallons. It is the means of punishing sin, and
it is appropriate that sin should thus be exactly measured by
something which 'goeth forth' from God. Possibly the shape
rather than the capacity is that of the ephah, so that it may be
rendered 'barrel.'

This is their resemblance. These words (as R. V. marg.) mean
in Hebrew 'this is their eye.' Not much help is obtained even
by twisting the word to mean 'resemblance.' Perhaps the words
are a gloss, and we must connect 'in all the land' with 'goeth
forth.' The Septuagint takes a somewhat similar Hebrew word,
and renders 'iniquity' (see R.V. marg.).

woman sitting in the midst of the ephah. And he said, 8
This is Wickedness ; and he cast her down into the midst
of the ephah : and he cast the weight of lead upon the
mouth thereof. Then lifted I up mine eyes, and saw, and 9
behold, there came forth two women, and the wind was in
their wings ; now they had wings like the wings of a stork :
and they lifted up the ephah between the earth and the
heaven. Then said I to the angel that talked with me, 10
Whither do these bear the ephah? And he said unto 11
me, To build her an house in the land of Shinar : and
when it is prepared, she shall be set there in her own
place.

---

7. there was lifted up a talent of lead. This was probably
done by the angel. The words are no longer his, but a paren-
thesis by the prophet telling of the next thing he saw. The
talent was a heavy weight of lead, but as the talent was 'round,'
so called from its shape, it may only mean 'round piece' (as R.V.
marg.), and this 'disk of lead' may be simply the heavy cover of
the barrel.

a woman. The wickedness of the land is thus personified.
She has already been seized and put in the ephah.

8. he cast her down, etc. Evidently wickedness still struggles
to get loose, even after her seizure, but Jehovah's angel makes sure
that she cannot get loose, by putting the cover on the ephah.

9. two women. It is only fair to the sex that, if wickedness
is a woman, it should also be women who remove her.

like the wings of a stork. The stork is common in Palestine,
and is a bird which is very strong on the wing. In its migrations
it flies very high, 'between the earth and the heaven.'

11. To build her an house in the land of Shinar. Wickedness
is deported to the land of Israel's traditional oppressor, for Shinar
means Babylonia (see Gen. xi. 2). She is there to be set in a
place where she may stay and flourish, for even her permanent
removal from their own land is not enough; she must find a
place among their enemies.

in her own place : i.e. the one that really suits her. But R.V.
marg. follows A.V. in rendering 'upon her own base,' i.e. in a
fixed position, perhaps still referring to the ephah.

It has been suggested that 'Wickedness' of *v.* 8 refers specially
to *idolatry*, as being the Jews' worst sin, and one to which they
were still tempted. Babylon would of course be a natural place
for it. This interpretation will explain why such stress is laid on
building her a house, i.e. a temple.

vi. 1–8. *The Eighth Vision. The Four
Chariots and their mission.*

6 And again I lifted up mine eyes, and saw, and behold,
there came four chariots out from between two mountains;
2 and the mountains were mountains of brass. In the first
chariot were red horses; and in the second chariot black
3 horses; and in the third chariot white horses; and in the
4 fourth chariot grisled bay horses. Then I answered and
said unto the angel that talked with me, What are these,
5 my lord? And the angel answered and said unto me,
These are the four winds of heaven, which go forth from

———————————

vi. 1–8. The last vision is very like the first one of the Four
Horsemen. But the chariots go forth to do more than report to
Jehovah. The use of chariots among the Jews seems to have been
exclusively for the purpose of warfare, and these chariots go to
the four quarters of the earth to defend or avenge Judah. The
one that went towards Babylonia is singled out as having taken
vengeance, and satisfied the justice of Jehovah.

1. from between two mountains. These mountains of brass
seem to be purely imaginary, possibly being a traditional means
of exit from heaven. Dr Barnes (*op. cit.* p. 51) notes that on
Babylonian seals the sun is represented as rising between two
mountains. The Septuagint puts 'mountains' for 'myrtles' in
the first vision, probably influenced by this one.

2. red horses, etc. The horses with their several colours
figure here again, and after *v.* 5 they are put instead of the
chariots. The only colour which is plainly symbolic is that of the
'black horses' which go to the dark north to punish Israel's worst
foe.

3. grisled bay horses: grisled is grey, but the Heb. means
'spotted' or dappled. The word for 'bay' may equally well be
rendered 'strong' (as R.V. marg.).

The later verses shew much confusion in the colours, but this
is not a point of importance.

5. These are the four winds of heaven. The chariots went
forth to the four winds, but can they be said actually to *be* the
winds? Some editors, by adding a letter, alter the sense to
'These are going forth *towards* the four winds of heaven, from
standing,' etc. Or we may read, as R.V. marg., 'the four spirits'
(cf. the spirits sent forth in 1 Kings xxii. 19–22, who likewise
presented themselves before Jehovah).

standing before the Lord of all the earth. *The chariot* 6
wherein are the black horses goeth forth toward the north
country ; and the white went forth after them ; and the
grisled went forth toward the south country. And the bay 7
went forth, and sought to go that they might walk to and
fro through the earth : and he said, Get you hence, walk
to and fro through the earth. So they walked to and fro
through the earth. Then cried he upon me, and spake 8
unto me, saying, Behold, they that go toward the north
country have quieted my spirit in the north country.

---

6. The chariot, etc. The words are simply 'the black horses
are going forth.'

the north country. See note on ii. 6 for the direction of
Babylonia.

the white went forth after them. This spoils the idea of the
four winds. It is better to understand '*behind* them' in another
sense, i.e. that, to one facing eastward (as the Jew did in thinking of the points of the compass), they turned to what was behind
them, viz. the west. The *white* horses may possibly be thus
turned towards Judah, because their colour is propitious, but it
has been suggested that the colour refers to the fairer peoples of
Europe.

7. the bay went forth. If the word means 'strong,' it may
explain why they were given the heavy task of patrolling the
whole earth. This great commission (as a world-wide protection
to Judah) is at their own request; they 'sought to go.'

8. cried he upon me. The expression is an archaic one, meaning 'he called to me.' The angel seems to be again the subject,
but Mitchell (*op. cit.* p. 181) maintains that it is Jehovah Himself. An interval has evidently elapsed before this verse, for at
least a part of the commission on which they started is now
fulfilled. But a vision need take no more account of time than
an ordinary dream.

have quieted my spirit: i.e. have satisfied my anger. Cf.
Ezek. v. 13, 'I will satisfy my fury upon them.' Thus the eighth
vision is like the seventh in closing with a judgment upon
Babylon.

It is uncertain whether the vision refers to the past or the
future. Does it look back to the judgment upon Babylon by its
capture by the Persians under Cyrus in 538? Or does it refer to
the revolt of Babylonia in this year of anarchy 520? The fact
that the later visions have pointed, not to the past, but to the
future, makes the last suggestion more likely.

9–15. HISTORICAL APPENDIX TO THE VISIONS.

9–11. *The prophet's reception of the deputation
from Babylon.*

9 And the word of the LORD came unto me, saying, Take
10 of them of the captivity, even of Heldai, of Tobijah, and

9–15. Several explanations of this difficult passage may be
given, and, for the sake of clearness, a brief summary of the chief
of them is given first.

(*a*) **9–12.** The prophet's action with regard to 'them of the
captivity.'

i. The exiles still at Babylon have sent a deputation to Jerusalem with silver and gold to help the builders. On the very day
of their arrival Zechariah summons them together and receives
their offering. With it he makes a crown, and uses it as a symbolic honour for the heads of the community.

ii. It is not a deputation, but some of their own community of
returned exiles, who are taken by Zechariah as witnesses and
sharers of his symbolic act. They go with him, on the day of his
visions, to the house of Josiah, in which they were living. Perhaps the latter was a goldsmith, and they all join with him in
making what the prophet asks for.

(*b*) **13–15.** The prophet's message when the crown is set on
Joshua's head.

i. There are really *two* crowns, as is stated in *v.* 11. One
is set on Joshua's head and the other on Zerubbabel's, and then
the latter is again told that as temple-builder he is to be the
'shoot' of the new Messianic kingdom. His name is suppressed
in *v.* 11, purposely made obscure, for fear of making the Persian
government suspicious that a rebellion is being attempted under
his kingship. In the case of a high-priest there is no need for
such caution. In *v.* 11, we must understand 'set them *upon
the head of Zerubbabel*, *and* upon the head of Joshua.' This
explanation is supported by the similar difficulties in *v.* 13 (see
note on that verse).

ii. There is only one crown (as in R.V. marg. in *v.* 14), the
plural being used in *v.* 11 to denote the circlets of which it was
composed. It is placed on the head of Joshua, by a tactful
effort on the part of Zechariah to prevent his being jealous of
Zerubbabel. Already Joshua has had to give way to his colleague
in the fourth vision (iii. 8), and so he is now given a share of the
honour, in the form of a crown which shall complete the mitre (cf.
iii. 5) in accordance with the rule of Exod. xxix. 6, ' Thou shalt put
the mitre upon his head, and put the holy crown upon the mitre.'

iii. The crown was not intended for Joshua at all, but for

of Jedaiah ; and come thou the same day, and go into the
house of Josiah the son of Zephaniah, whither they are
come from Babylon ; yea, take *of them* silver and gold, 11
and make crowns, and set them upon the head of Joshua
the son of Jehozadak, the high priest ;

Zerubbabel. But in a later age, when the latter had entirely
disappointed Messianic expectations, and the high-priest led the
nation instead of a descendant of David's line, the text of *v.* 11
was altered accordingly, and 'Joshua the son of Jehozadak' was
substituted for 'Zerubbabel the son of Shealtiel.' A solution may
be arrived at by omitting all of *v.* 11 that comes after the word
'crowns.'

Perhaps (*a*) i. and (*b*) i. or ii. are to be preferred. Dr Barnes
takes (*a*) i. and (*b*) ii., without suggesting any other explanation
(*op. cit.* pp. 54, 55).

If a new suggestion may be allowed with regard to the persons
of Zerubbabel and Joshua in (*b*), why should not *Joshua* be called
the 'Branch' here, as Zerubbabel was in iii. 8 ? In *v.* 12 it is
really 'Behold *a* man whose name is the Branch.' It was he who
built the temple along with his colleague ; one has already received
Messianic honour ; now it is Joshua's turn, 'and *he* shall...rule upon
his throne' (*v.* 13). The word 'both' at the end of *v.* 13 comes
awkwardly, but the suggestion to omit it has been made.

9. the word of the Lord: no longer spoken through the
angelic medium.

10. Take of them of the captivity, etc. In what sense is he
to 'take of them'? Possibly the object is the one found in *v.* 11,
'take of them silver and gold.' But this is very clumsy, and it is
more likely to mean 'take some of them.' The **captivity** or
golah was the regular post-exilic name for those who had been in
exile at Babylon.

even of Heldai. The name causes some difficulty. In *v.* 14 it
appears as Helem (see note). Both are perhaps corrupt forms of
the original name.

the same day. Either the day on which the deputation arrived
in Jerusalem, or the same day as the visions (i. 7).

go into the house of Josiah. Either it was he who had given
hospitality to those mentioned in the verse ; or else, following the
Septuagint, and also taking **house** in the correct sense of 'household' we may render 'go in unto the household of Josiah...which
have come from Babylon.' In this case it will mean that the
deputation consisted of members of the family of Josiah.

11. crowns, and set them. Cf. *v.* 14. The rendering of the
R.V. marg. is 'a crown, and set it.'

12-15. *The prophet's message when he has given the crowns.*

12 and speak unto him, saying, Thus speaketh the LORD of hosts, saying, Behold, the man whose name is the Branch; and he shall grow up out of his place, and he shall build
13 the temple of the LORD : even he shall build the temple of the LORD ; and he shall bear the glory, and shall sit and rule upon his throne ; and he shall be a priest upon his throne : and the counsel of peace shall be between them
14 both.   And the crowns shall be to Helem, and to Tobijah,

---

12. unto him. Either Joshua or Zerubbabel, according to the explanation taken of the previous verse.

whose name is the Branch. His identity is still concealed, but must have been quite obvious. But it must be remembered that Zerubbabel had not yet proved himself to be the man. The expectation is of the future. For the title see note on iii. 8.

he shall grow up out of his place. There is a play on the words. It is promised that the shoot shall 'shoot up.' But the verb may perhaps be impersonal, as the R.V. marg., which says of the 'Bud' that 'it shall bud forth under him,' i.e. success shall come in his reign. If **out of his place** means more than 'in his place,' it may suggest that Zerubbabel is to rise suddenly to a far higher position.

13. he shall build the temple. Cf. iv. 9, 'his hands shall also finish it.'

he shall bear the glory: or rather 'he shall bear majesty,' i.e. he shall assume the position of Messianic king, as a reward for his building.

and he shall be a priest upon his throne. There are thus shewn to be two thrones, as well as two crowns, for the civil and religious leaders. This suits with the word 'both' at the end of the verse, but it requires the rendering of the R.V. marg., i.e. '*there* shall be a priest,' etc. And if we render 'upon his throne' by 'beside his throne,' the passage becomes clear. Some would insert the word 'Joshua' instead of '*he* shall be.' In any case, it is he who is intended.

the counsel of peace. There was a risk that their dual control might bring the two men into rivalry. See (*b*) ii. in note on p. 62.

14. The crowns are to be kept in the temple, as a solemn reminder, while the men who gave them shall gain blessing for their deed.

and to Jedaiah, and to Hen the son of Zephaniah, for a
memorial in the temple of the LORD. And they that are 15
far off shall come and build in the temple of the LORD,
and ye shall know that the LORD of hosts hath sent me
unto you. And *this* shall come to pass, if ye will diligently
obey the voice of the LORD your God.

---

the crowns (or **crown** as R.V. marg.). See note on *v.* 11.

Helem. See note on Heldai, *v.* 10. Possibly neither Heldai
nor Helem (which appears here in place of it) is a proper name.

to Hen the son of Zephaniah. The word Hen here takes the
place of 'Josiah the son of Zephaniah' in *v.* 10. It can hardly be
a mutilated form of Josiah. The alternative is to translate it, like
Helem above, as a common noun, i.e. as R.V. marg., 'for the
kindness of the son of Zephaniah.' If the latter alternative is
chosen, it supports the theory that Josiah already lived in Jerusalem, and was the host who entertained the deputation, or at
whose house these returned exiles were living. But if 'Hen' be
simply equivalent to 'Josiah,' he is thus coupled with the others,
and this fits with the theory that he was one of the deputation
from Babylon, which consisted of the family of Zephaniah.

15. they that are far off, etc. This seems to be a promise
that the Jews still in Babylon shall return in larger numbers and
help in the work. If the men in the preceding verse were a
deputation, their coming would suggest the possibility of a 'return' on a grand scale. But viii. 22 justifies the suggestion that
other nations are included in these 'far off' ones.

And this shall come to pass. There is no word for **this** in
Heb. The clause therefore refers, not to the preceding promises,
but to something that is to follow. It looks as if the sentence
was broken off in the middle, either through some early corrup-
tion in the text, or because the last part of Zechariah's prophecies
of the 24th day of the 11th month was never completed in writing.

vii.-viii. We have in these chapters a valuable addition to
these prophecies. Haggai's stopped short in the great year of
crisis 520. But Zechariah by being called upon to prophesy
again two years later, gives us a further picture of Jerusalem
when the building of the temple was just half finished. They
may be roughly divided into two, ch. vii., giving warnings from
the past, and ch. viii., giving encouragements for the future.
vii. 1 gives a fixed date for the prophecy, but several times after-
ward we are told that 'the word of the LORD of hosts came.'
This need not have been all on the same day. But the two
chapters must certainly be regarded as a unity; for in vii. 3 a
question is propounded to the prophet to which his prophecy

III. The Third Prophecy. Warnings from the
PAST AND ENCOURAGEMENTS FOR THE FUTURE.

vii. 1-3. *The occasion of the prophecy.*

7 And it came to pass in the fourth year of king Darius,
that the word of the LORD came unto Zechariah in the
2 fourth *day* of the ninth month, even in Chislev. Now
they of Beth-el had sent Sharezer and Regem-melech,
3 and their men, to intreat the favour of the LORD, *and* to
speak unto the priests of the house of the LORD of hosts,

---

is meant to be the answer, but it is only in viii. 18 that he gives
a direct reply.

vii. 1. in the fourth year: i.e. 518, two years after the last
prophecy. The ninth month is given its Babylonian name Chislev
in Neh. i. 1.

2-3. The prophet breaks silence as the result of a direct request. A deputation has come (cf. vi. 9) to ask the spiritual
authorities at Jerusalem whether they are doing right in still
observing fasts which were kept during the exile, in commemoration of some of the dreadful events of the time when Jerusalem
was besieged and taken (588–586).

2. they of Beth-el. The list in Ezr. ii. of the returned exiles
gives several as being of Beth-el (*v.* 28). And the men of Beth-el
are mentioned in later time (Neh. xi. 31) as among those who
did not come into Jerusalem to live. But was it Beth-el which
sent the deputation? See the next note.

Sharezer and Regem-melech, and their men. The Heb. is
difficult. Note that Sharezer (Protect the King) is a Babylonian
name, and Regem-melech (King's Friend) Hebrew; and that the
words that follow may be translated 'and *his* men.' Also in *v.* 3 the
question is in the singular, 'should *I* weep?' It looks as if there
was only one man who headed the mission. We may read either
(1) 'had sent Sharezer, even Regem-melech, and his men,' or
(2), as R.V. marg., 'even Sharezer, had sent Regem-melech and
his men.' But, in view of the difficulties of these names, can we
be sure that the words are right 'now *Beth-el* had sent'? It does
not seem a very likely place for a mission to be sent from at this
time. It has been suggested that the word is really 'Bel,' giving
the compound Babylonian name Belsharezer (O Bel, protect the
king!). The sense will now be that Belsharezer had sent Regem-
melech. If we would know the place whence the mission came,
it is most likely to be Babylon. (Cf. vi. 9 for a deputation
thence.)

and to the prophets, saying, Should I weep in the fifth month,
separating myself, as I have done these so many years?

*4–7. The first message. They still need the prophetic
teaching that fasting is useless without spirituality.*

Then came the word of the LORD of hosts unto me, saying, 4
Speak unto all the people of the land, and to the priests, 5
saying, When ye fasted and mourned in the fifth and in
the seventh *month*, even these seventy years, did ye at all

---

3. Should I weep in the fifth month, etc. To 'weep' is to
keep a fast in demonstrative Jewish fashion. The seventh day of
the fifth month is given in 2 Kings xxv. 8 as the fatal day when
the temple was destroyed by the conquering Babylonians. From
586 till 518 the exiles seem to have kept a fast in memory of it
('even these seventy years,' *v.* 5). Now that the new temple is
half built, they naturally are beginning to wonder whether this
sad commemoration may stop.

Many explanations have been attempted for the coming of the
mission in the ninth month, when they had kept the fast only
four months previously. But note that when Zechariah gives them
their answer in viii. 19, he mentions other fasts along with it,
including that of the *tenth* month. Perhaps the question was
meant to refer to all the fasts of the exile, but the event commemorated in the fifth month was the most important in relation
to the temple.

4. Although the only date is the one given in vii. 1, there
seem to be four prophecies included in these two chapters, each
beginning with the statement that the word of the LORD came to
Zechariah (vii. 4, vii. 8, viii. 1 and viii. 18). We may therefore
divide the sections accordingly. The general theme is the restoration of the Jews to Jehovah's favour, but each oracle of the series
regards it from a different point of view.

5. Speak unto all the people, etc. The prophet uses the
opportunity given by the questioner, but addresses his reply far
more widely. It is a message for all, but specially to the priests,
who had control of the fasts.

in the seventh month. This fast probably commemorated the
murder of Gedaliah, the governor who was left in Judah by
Nebuchadrezzar in 586 after the destruction of Jerusalem. For
the full story of his murder at Mizpah by Ishmael, see Jerem.
xl. 13–xli. 2. The result was that the 'remnant of Judah' fled
into Egypt to escape the wrath of Nebuchadrezzar. Some would
connect this fast with the Day of Atonement, which in post-exilic
times was on the tenth day of the seventh month.

6 fast unto me, even to me? And when ye eat, and when ye
   drink, do not ye eat for yourselves, and drink for your-
7 selves? *Should ye* not *hear* the words which the LORD
   hath cried by the former prophets, when Jerusalem was
   inhabited and in prosperity, and the cities thereof round
   about her, and the South and the lowland were inhabited?

8-14. *The second message. The lack of justice and sympathy is still the explanation of national disaster and
   desolation.*

8   And the word of the LORD came unto Zechariah, saying,

---

did ye at all fast unto me. The idea of humiliation before
God did not enter into their fasts, which were simply lamentations
for national disasters. They were therefore useless in God's eyes.

6. do not ye eat for yourselves, etc. This must mean that it
does not matter whether they eat or abstain, for in either case it
has no connexion with God, and only concerns themselves. The
eating may refer to the share of a sacrifice which was given to
the sacrificers (Deut. xii. 5–7).

7. by the former prophets: i.e. those before the exile, cf. i. 4.
The message they had so often given was that mere outward
ceremonial was useless unless the heart was turned to God. See
note on *vv.* 10, 11.

the South and the lowland: i.e. the Negeb, in the south of
Judah, and the Shephelah or western lowlands of Judah towards
the Philistine plains.

8-14. As the text stands, this is a further message, which
carries on the reference to the former prophets, but proceeds to
apply their teaching to other things besides fasting. It is lack of
true religion that is their curse throughout. As their duty to God
has been lacking in reality, so has their duty to their neighbour
been unfulfilled through heartless selfishness. As their fasts have
been for themselves, so has it been with their whole lives.
Zechariah therefore repeats the familiar prophetic warnings as
to the result of such conduct.

But it has been suggested that *v.* 8 is to be omitted, as a later
interpolation, inserted by a scribe who did not realise that the
message of *vv.* 9–10 was that of the former prophets. In this
case, *v.* 9 does not begin a new section, but gives 'the words
which the LORD hath cried by the former prophets,' introduced
in *v.* 7. It is urged in support of this view, that it is unlikely
that the prophet himself would say in *v.* 8 'unto Zechariah,'
instead of 'unto me.' But this is already found in vii. 1.

8. See note above.

Thus hath the LORD of hosts spoken, saying, Execute 9
true judgement, and shew mercy and compassion every
man to his brother: and oppress not the widow, nor the 10
fatherless, the stranger, nor the poor; and let none of you
imagine evil against his brother in your heart. But they 11
refused to hearken, and pulled away the shoulder, and
stopped their ears, that they should not hear. Yea, they 12
made their hearts as an adamant stone, lest they should
hear the law, and the words which the LORD of hosts had
sent by his spirit by the hand of the former prophets:
therefore came there great wrath from the LORD of hosts.
And it came to pass that, as he cried, and they would not 13
hear; so they shall cry, and I will not hear, said the LORD
of hosts ; but I will scatter them with a whirlwind among 14

---

9. Thus hath *Jehovah* **of hosts spoken.** Whichever of the
above interpretations be taken, these words refer to the *past*
utterances of Jehovah through His prophets. For instances of such
a message see Amos v. 12, 16; Hos. vi. 6; Is. i. 17; Jer. vii. 6.
The language of the prophets is frequently echoed in Deutero-
nomy (e.g. xvi. 19, 20; xxiv. 17).

10. oppress not, etc. This was a favourite injunction, and is
also found in Exod. xxii. 21, 22.

let none of you imagine evil: a deeper as well as a wider ap-
plication of their duty.

11-12. Zechariah here describes the way the prophet's message
was received. They began with indifference, but proceeded to
avoid the messengers, and finally were completely and purposely
hardened to anything purporting to come from God.

11. pulled away the shoulder: i.e. like an animal that refuses
to submit to the yoke. The R.V. marg. ('turned a stubborn
shoulder') makes this a little plainer.

12. hear the law: Heb. *torah*, i.e. the 'direction' or instruction which comes from God, chiefly through His priests, but also
through His prophets. Cf. Hagg. ii. 11.

by his spirit: i.e. the power from God which inspired the
prophets to give their message. Cf. Neh. ix. 30.

therefore came there great wrath, etc. He here begins to
describe the result of their refusal to listen to the message. God
shewed His wrath by treating them as they had treated Him.

14. but I will scatter them with a whirlwind. As he is
giving the result of the past, many would turn this into a past
tense, by a very trifling alteration of the Hebrew. The phrase
translates a single word, meaning 'toss or whirl them away.'

all the nations whom they have not known. Thus the land
was desolate after them, that no man passed through nor
returned : for they laid the pleasant land desolate.

viii. 1–17. *The third message. A series of promises concerning the restoration of the prosperity of Jerusalem.*

8   And the word of the LORD of hosts came *to me*, saying,
2 Thus saith the LORD of hosts : I am jealous for Zion with
great jealousy, and I am jealous for her with great fury.
3 Thus saith the LORD : I am returned unto Zion, and will
dwell in the midst of Jerusalem : and Jerusalem shall be
called The city of truth ; and the mountain of the LORD
4 of hosts The holy mountain. Thus saith the LORD of

---

that no man passed through nor returned. The natural sense
seems to be 'so that there was none coming or going.' But
Dr Barnes would explain 'so that no one willingly passed through
or returned by that desolate way again' (*op. cit.* p. 63).

for they laid the pleasant land desolate. The result of the
exile was the desolation of a land once so fertile as to deserve
the title of 'land of desire' (R.V. marg.).

viii. 1–17. This is the next section into which the prophecy
is divided, the break being marked by the words of *v.* 1, which
occur again in *v.* 18. If a further subdivision is made after *v.* 8,
the earlier part is found to refer to the future only, whereas the
promises of *vv.* 9-17 are a series of contrasts with the past.

Driver (*op. cit.* p. 220) styles the whole of ch. viii. 'A decalogue of promises,' the whole forming a unity in which the formula
'Thus saith the LORD of hosts' is repeated ten times.

2. Zion. See note on i. 14 (where the form of the words is
almost the same).

3. I am returned. After two years the promise of i. 3 is regarded as fulfilled.

The city of truth, i.e. of truthfulness, or rather 'faithfulness'
towards Jehovah.

The holy mountain. In Is. lxvi. 20 Jerusalem is so called, so
the word seems to refer here to the whole city, and not only to
the hill on which the temple stood.

4-5. These verses give a beautiful picture of a prosperous and
peaceful city, well filled with a happy and long-lived population.
The returned exiles were pioneers who knew little of family life ;
children were scarce among them, and the life they had passed
gave to but few the likelihood of living to old age.

hosts : There shall yet old men and old women dwell in
the streets of Jerusalem, every man with his staff in his
hand for very age. And the streets of the city shall be full 5
of boys and girls playing in the streets thereof. Thus saith 6
the LORD of hosts : If it be marvellous in the eyes of the
remnant of this people in those days, should it also be
marvellous in mine eyes? saith the LORD of hosts. Thus 7
saith the LORD of hosts : Behold, I will save my people
from the east country, and from the west country: and 8
I will bring them, and they shall dwell in the midst of
Jerusalem ; and they shall be my people, and I will be
their God, in truth and in righteousness. Thus saith the 9
LORD of hosts : Let your hands be strong, ye that hear in
these days these words from the mouth of the prophets,
which were in the day that the foundation of the house of
the LORD of hosts was laid, even the temple, that it might

---

4. dwell in the streets of Jerusalem : or rather 'sit in the
broad places.' So also with *v.* 5, with which we may compare
the 'children sitting in the market places' in Matth. xi. 16, 17.

6. The meaning is that 'with God nothing is impossible.' To
the Jews the picture thus drawn seemed too good to be true.

7-8. The next promise in the 'decalogue' is a still wider one,
though it helps to explain the last. Scattered Jews from all over
the world will come to swell the population of the holy city.

7. and from the west country : lit. the country of the setting
sun. The phrase is probably a general one for the whole earth,
but if the 'west' has any special reference it must be Egypt.

8. they shall be my people, etc. An echo of words of promise
often used by Jeremiah (e.g. vii. 23) and Ezekiel (e.g. xi. 20).

9-17. The promises of these verses set forth the future as a
contrast with the past, but conditions for their fulfilment are laid
down.

9. Let your hands be strong. Now that the temple is half
completed, he repeats the encouragement given by Haggai when
they had decided to begin it (Hagg. ii. 4).

from the mouth of the prophets, etc. This seems to imply
that there were other prophets besides himself and Haggai in the
period after the Return. But they are the only two mentioned in
Ezra v. The words **which were in the day** may be translated
'which were spoken concerning the day.' If so, their subject is
these words, and not 'the prophets.' In this case, 'these
words' may refer to his own echoes of the language of the
former prophets, such as he has just given in the previous verse.

10 be built. For before those days there was no hire for man,
nor any hire for beast ; neither was there any peace to him
that went out or came in because of the adversary : for I set
11 all men every one against his neighbour. But now I will
not be unto the remnant of this people as in the former days,
12 saith the LORD of hosts. For *there shall be* the seed of
peace ; the vine shall give her fruit, and the ground shall
give her increase, and the heavens shall give their dew ;
and I will cause the remnant of this people to inherit all
13 these things. And it shall come to pass that, as ye were
a curse among the nations, O house of Judah and house
of Israel, so will I save you, and ye shall be a blessing :
14 fear not, *but* let your hands be strong. For thus saith the
LORD of hosts : As I thought to do evil unto you, when
your fathers provoked me to wrath, saith the LORD of
15 hosts, and I repented not ; so again have I thought in

---

that it might be built. This is either the actual promise made
by the prophets, or the result of what they spoke.

10. In this verse are combined the two chief obstacles to the
rebuilding of the temple. The first was the scarcity of the times,
as told at length by Haggai (see i. 6 and ii. 16, 17). The other
was the opposition of the adversaries in the country round, of
which the prophets tell us nothing except in this verse, but it is
given in full in Ezra iv. and v. But a third obstacle is added at the
end of the verse, **and** (not 'for') **I set all men every one against
his neighbour,** i.e. there were internal dissensions *beside* the
trouble caused by those outside.

there was no hire, etc. : i.e. there was a shortage both of wages
and of work.

11. as in the former days : i.e. the preceding years since the
Return.

12. This follows Haggai's prediction (ii. 19) that the building
of the temple will bring an era of prosperity. There shall come
such harvests as peace brings (or possibly, the sowing of peace
itself), and instead of blasting and mildew and hail (Hagg. ii. 17),
God will give them good seasons.

13. ye were a curse among the nations : i.e. recognised by
them as the objects of God's curse. Now they will be regarded
as shewing what blessings He can give to men.

14-15. The fact that God kept His word in earlier time by
sending punishment in spite of their adversity, is a guarantee
that they need not fear that He will fail to fulfil the blessing now
promised.

these days to do good unto Jerusalem and to the house of
Judah : fear ye not. These are the things that ye shall 16
do ; Speak ye every man the truth with his neighbour ;
execute the judgement of truth and peace in your gates :
and let none of you imagine evil in your hearts against his 17
neighbour ; and love no false oath : for all these are things
that I hate, saith the LORD.

18-23. *The fourth message. Fasts shall be turned into*
feasts, in a reign of joy and gladness.

And the word of the LORD of hosts came unto me, 18
saying, Thus saith the LORD of hosts : The fast of the 19
fourth *month*, and the fast of the fifth, and the fast of the

---

16-17. They need not fear, but there are certain moral conditions which God demands from them in return, which include
that justice and compassion which the former prophets demanded
of their forefathers (see vii. 9-10). The addition of the 'false
oath' recalls the vision of the flying roll, where to the thief as a
type of sinners is added 'him that sweareth falsely by my name'
(see note on v. 4).

16. the judgement of truth and peace. Truth is to figure in
their courts as well as in their conversation. 'The judgement of
peace' seems to be such as would lead to peace, impartial justice
which no one could quarrel with ; cf. 'the counsel of peace' in
vi. 13.

in your gates: for the gate of the city was always the place
both of justice and of business (see e.g. Ruth iv. 1).

17. false oath. This was evidently a special sin of Zechariah's
own time, but the law makes frequent reference to it, and it of
course appears in the third of the Ten Commandments.

18-19. Once again 'the word of Jehovah' comes, and at
length Zechariah gives an answer to the query (vii. 3) which was
the occasion of the prophecy.

If they fulfil the conditions of the promised blessing, they may
turn these fasts and others like them into happy festivals.

19. The fast of the fourth month, etc. This fast, and that of
the tenth month, are mentioned here for the first time.

On the ninth day of the *fourth* month of 586, Nebuchadrezzar
made a breach in the walls of Jerusalem, which caused the entry
of the Babylonians, and the useless flight of Zedekiah and his
army (2 Kings xxv. 3-5).

On the tenth day of the *tenth* month, a year and a half previously, in 588, the siege of Jerusalem began (2 Kings xxv. 1).

seventh, and the fast of the tenth, shall be to the house of
Judah joy and gladness, and cheerful feasts ; therefore
20 love truth and peace. Thus saith the LORD of hosts: *It
shall* yet *come to pass,* that there shall come peoples,
21 and the inhabitants of many cities : and the inhabitants of
one *city* shall go to another, saying, Let us go speedily
to intreat the favour of the LORD, and to seek the LORD
22 of hosts : I will go also. Yea, many peoples and strong
nations shall come to seek the LORD of hosts in Jerusalem
23 and to intreat the favour of the LORD. Thus saith the
LORD of hosts : In those days *it shall come to pass,* that
ten men shall take hold, out of all the languages of the
nations, shall even take hold of the skirt of him that is
a Jew, saying, We will go with you, for we have heard
that God is with you.

For the other fasts, see notes on vii. 3 and 5. It will be noted
that, with the exception of the fast of the tenth month, the fasts
refer to the order of events between the fourth and seventh
months of the year 586.

cheerful feasts: or cheerful seasons. They will do well still
to remember these days, but with a new thankfulness which may
actually turn them into festivals.

therefore love truth and peace : because these are the conditions of the change (*v.* 16).

20–22. The prosperity of Jerusalem will attract the outside
nations (see *v.* 13), so that they will invite each other to join in a
pilgrimage thither to honour Jehovah and His house. This is as
far as the prophets attained by way of missionary ideal, and it is
somewhat in advance of Haggai (ii. 7). See note on ii. 11, and
Introd. p. 27.

21. Let us go speedily. The Heb. does not express speed
but urgency, 'Let us go, go.'

23. The final promise of the 'decalogue' is quaint as well as
picturesque. Men of nations speaking other languages, in a proportion as great as ten to one, shall attach themselves to each
Jew in order that he may lead them to where God dwells in His
holy house.

take hold of the skirt : i.e. the 'border' or edge of his robe.

God is with you. A fine phrase with which to conclude the
prophecy. It has been noted that instead of using the word
Jehovah or Lord (as elsewhere in this book) the prophet here puts
into the mouths of these Gentiles the word for God (Elohim)
which they might use already for their own gods.

INTRODUCTION TO ZECHARIAH,
Chapters IX–XIV

§ 1. Reasons for regarding these chapters as not by Zechariah.

The suggestion was made as long ago as the seventeenth century that there is a change of authorship after ch. viii. Since then, there has been an increasing tendency to accept this as a fact, and many new arguments have been urged in support of it. It is certainly not an unwarranted attitude to adopt, and its likelihood has been increased by the modern acceptance of the fact that chs. xl.–lxvi. of Isaiah are not by that prophet, but probably represent the work of more than one author, whose words have become attached to those of the well-known book of Isaiah.

The chief reasons may briefly be summarised as follows:

(a) *These chapters are unlike the rest in style and language.* Zechariah wrote in prose. But ix. 1–10 is a poem, and there are traces of metre in the other chapters too. The vocabulary differs from that of Zechariah. His favourite expressions are absent; e.g. 'saith the LORD of hosts' (seventeen times) does not occur at all. On the other hand, expressions characteristic of the last chapters are rare in the earlier ones ; e.g. 'in that day,' as referring to the future (eighteen times in the later chapters, but only three in the earlier). Zechariah was a follower of the 'former prophets,' and often echoes their language. The later chapters make no reference to them, and quote from different prophets. There are no parallels in them with Zechariah's fellow-prophet Haggai.

(b) *They are unlike in historical references.* There are

no dates affixed, as is the case with Zechariah and Haggai. Zerubbabel and Joshua are not mentioned, but the rulers of Judah are denounced as cruel and neglectful (xi. 4 ff.). The prophets are now not a help but a degradation (xiii. 2–6). The building of the temple is unmentioned, and instead of the immediate glory of Jerusalem, its capture by the Gentiles is described as coming before its deliverance (xii. 2 ff., xiv. 1–7). The typical foe is not Babylon, but smaller and nearer cities, such as Damascus, Tyre, and the towns of the Philistines, and conflict with the Greeks is foreshadowed. Beside Judah, the northern kingdom is mentioned as existent, generally under the name of Ephraim.

(*c*) *They are unlike in outlook.* To begin with, the author's relation to God is different There is no longer an angel as intermediary, but, like the prophets generally, he speaks as the direct mouthpiece of Jehovah. His pictures of the Messianic age are quite different from Zechariah's. They are not of the practical kind, connected with men like Zerubbabel, but they are of apocalyptic nature, revelations of marvels wrought by divine interposition. Jerusalem is to be the centre of salvation not because the temple invites all men to worship, and its restoration has brought the blessings of prosperity and good harvests, but because God comes down to fight for it like a man. The sobriety of Zechariah (see p. 30) is exchanged for an extravagance which delights in marvels. The turning of mountains into a plain is no longer simply expressive of the smoothing away of difficulties. The Mount of Olives will be cleft in two (perhaps in order that the people may escape by means of the chasm), and the whole contour of the country will be miraculously altered (xiv. 4, 5). There is no moral appeal to the people, either to return to Jehovah, or to deal kindly with each other, which was an essential part of Zechariah's message. And there is a certain heartlessness which is very different from the human touches which the earlier chapters contain.

But in spite of these and similar arguments, it is still possible to believe that Zechariah wrote the whole book, and this is the conclusion arrived at by Van Hoonacker (*op. cit.* pp. 657 ff.). He accounts for the difference in style and language by the fact that Zechariah in chs. ix. ff. is dealing with altogether different subjects. The altered historical allusions may be due to the later date of writing, when the temple is already built. And as for the change of outlook, there is one important characteristic in which this is not the case. Zechariah, according to Van Hoonacker's interpretation of the visions, had a remarkable capacity for projecting himself into the circumstances of times other than his own (see p. 35), and the same thing is seen in the later chapters. For much appears to date from before the exile, when Judah had different foes, and when Israel was still in existence to the north of her; and yet the date is really post-exilic.

The student will see that there is an interesting problem, which has not been finally decided, and therefore its solution must not be wholly prejudged. But the probability is on the side of composite authorship.

§ 2. THEORIES OF THE ORIGIN AND DATE OF THESE CHAPTERS.

If Zechariah was not their author, how and when were they written? This is certainly a question which has not been fully answered. But an interest in it is at once created when we find that the dates which have been assigned to them vary to the extent of 500 years, between the eighth and the second or third centuries B.C. This divergence is caused by the strange fact that, when an attempt is made to refer the language to some particular era, it appears to apply to circumstances and events which are separated by centuries. For example, the hostility of Syrians, Phoenicians, and Philistines seems to imply that these nations had not yet been reduced to subjection. But in 734 B.C. they were made part of the Assyrian empire. The earthquake in Uzziah's days, which took place a little before that date, is referred to in xiv. 5 as if it might be a recent event. And if 'Ephraim' (which in the other prophets frequently stands for the Northern kingdom of Israel) is not yet destroyed, but still possessed of fighting strength (ix. 10, 13) it seems to imply a date before the captivity of the ten tribes in 722. But, on the other hand, there is a series of passages which point to a date subsequent to the destruction of Jerusalem in 586 and the return of the Judaean exiles. For example, the statement that God will protect His house, so that no oppressor shall pass through them *any more* (ix. 8), shews that Jerusalem had once fallen; and that He will 'bring again' the house of Joseph (x. 6) shews that the ten tribes were then in captivity. There is indeed one sentence which has made some editors decide on a far later date. In ix. 13 is the promise 'I will stir up thy sons, O Zion, against thy sons, O Greece.' It is argued that, if Greece is regarded as a world-power, whose domination shall be overthrown, this must be after the Greeks conquered the Persians and succeeded to their empire. This they did through the great victory of Alexander the Great at Issus in 333. The question remains as to how long after this the writer lived. It is declared in xiv. 2 that Jerusalem should be taken, and some have seen the fulfilment of this in the capture of the city by Ptolemy Philopator in 217.

The above outline is sufficient to shew that most of the conclusions thus reached depend upon laying stress on certain of the references, and allowing them more weight than those which seem to contradict them. The chief theories which have been put forward may be summarised thus:

(i) The prophecy dates from the eighth century, just after Amos prophesied in Jeroboam II's reign, when the nations which threatened them were the same (Zech. ix. 1–7 and Amos i. 3, 6, 9). The author was in that case an older contemporary of Isaiah,

(ii) It is of the seventh century, of the time of Jeremiah (who has himself been suggested as the author), when the death of Josiah at Megiddo was still remembered, as it seems to be referred to when there is wailing in the plain of Megiddon (xii. 11). The 'three shepherds' of xi. 8, who were so unworthy to rule, were the kings who followed, Jehoahaz, Jehoiakim and Jehoiachin; while the shepherd who should be smitten (and the sheep scattered) (xiii. 7) is Zedekiah, the last king of Judah.

(iii) It is of the sixth century, shortly after the prophecies of i.–viii. It has already been stated that Van Hoonacker not only accepts this view, but maintains that Zechariah himself was the author, some time after his other chapters. Dr Barnes recognises the differences of style and tone, and holds that i.–viii. were written by 'Zechariah the prophet,' and the rest by a follower of his, whom he calls 'Zechariah the disciple.' This is a great help towards explaining why this anonymous prophecy is included in the same book. For his arguments, see *op. cit.* pp. xviii.–xxii.

(iv) It is of the fifth century, shortly before the coming of Nehemiah in 444, and the building of the walls which secured Jerusalem against enemies. This places the book just before Malachi, which is its place in the O.T. And there is a further link. Ch. ix. begins with 'The burden of the word of the LORD.' So does ch. xii., where the second part of the prophecy begins. The only other place the expression occurs is in Mal. i. 1. (See note on xii. 1.)

(v) It is of the fourth century, just after the battle of Issus, in 333, when the Greek advance was threatening and Tyre had not yet fallen before Alexander, but was about to do so. 'The Lord will dispossess her' (ix. 4).

(vi) It is of the third century, and the references to Syria and Phoenicia along with the Greeks (in ix.) suggest the time of the Seleucid dynasty which inherited part of Alexander's empire. Some of it may be after the taking of Jerusalem in 217. We may pass over the suggestions of a still later date, connected with the period of the Maccabees.

The whole question is still further complicated by the fact that chs. ix.–xiv. have been thought not to form a unity in themselves, but to consist of distinct prophecies dating from different periods. One thing is quite clear. The six chapters consist of two sections of practically equal length.

(*a*) Chs. ix.–xi., with which must be included ch. xiii. 7–9, which reverts to the 'shepherds' of ch. xi.

(*b*) Chs. xii.–xiv., with the exception of xiii. 7–9.

Some editors subdivide these sections, and regard the prophecy as a growth, to which new sections were added in various periods. Mitchell (*op. cit.*) gives his conclusions as follows (and Driver seems to endorse them):

(*a*) ix. 1–10 written soon after Issus in 333.

(*b*) ix. 11 xi. 3 added to it in the reign of Ptolemy III (247–222).

(*c*) xi. 4–17 and xiii. 7–9 added by a third writer, who gives a pessimistic picture.

(*d*) xii. 1–xiii. 6 and xiv. added about the same time by a fourth writer, giving a more optimistic picture, and couched in apocalyptic language.

§ 3. THE VIEW WHICH IS MADE THE BASIS OF THE COMMENTARY WHICH FOLLOWS.

Readers are recommended to test the above theories for themselves in the light of the actual language of the prophecy. Chs. ix.–xiv. should be read rapidly through both before and after studying § 2. A final solution of the problem is still so far distant that it is quite legitimate for them to draw their own conclusions. But in any case they will expect some definite line to be adopted in the present writer's notes on the text. We will proceed to consider the chief considerations by which it has been arrived at.

(*a*) *There need not have been more than one author, but that author was not Zechariah.*

In spite of Van Hoonacker's contention, the points of

difference are far more numerous than those of agreement with the author of chs. i.–viii., and we may therefore decide that they are not his work. Moreover, as some of the arguments relate to the difference between the circumstances of his time and those set forth in these chapters, we may regard them as not written in his generation.

But, although two sections are clearly recognisable in the last six chapters, this does not warrant the conclusion that they were written by different prophets. The fact that the metaphor of the 'shepherds' of ch. xi. is introduced again in ch. xiii. 7–9, in itself strongly suggests that the author is the same. And the ingenious theories which regard the chapters as a patchwork, to which one prophet after another added his little contribution, are too uncertain for acceptance.

(*b*) *The author lived at a date subsequent to the Return from the Exile.*

A man may easily adapt his language to that of an earlier age, and refer to things which belong to a great and historic past. But if, intermingled with language which belonged to his predecessors in the prophetic office, he refers to what certainly belongs to a subsequent era, we must assign to him the later date. Indications which these chapters contain point us to a time when the return from exile had already taken place. And if their author was not contemporary with Zechariah, he must have lived still later.

(*c*) *The reference to 'Greece' is not enough to prove that he wrote after the rise of a Grecian empire in the East in about* 330.

For the arguments which lead to this conclusion, the reader is referred to Dr Barnes—*op. cit.* pp. xv.–xviii. It is a different matter in 1 Maccabees viii. 18, where it is the *kingdom* of the Greeks that is spoken of. Here it is simply the 'sons of Javan' (Greece), and the passage is on a level with passages like Gen. x. 2, where 'Javan' is one of the sons of Japheth, and Isaiah lxvi. 19, where those that escape are to be sent on a mission 'to Tubal, and Javan, to the isles afar off, that have not heard my fame.' The Hebrew word Javan or Yavan comes from 'Iavones,' the old Greek form of Ionians. It was these Ionian Greeks who settled in Asia Minor, and were well known to the Eastern world, especially in the later years of the reign of Darius, against whose authority they revolted in 499. There is no suggestion in Zech. ix. 13 that the Greeks have left the Mediterranean and founded a new empire by a hostile advance eastwards. The passage gives the promise of a great Jewish empire, spreading apparently from the Euphrates to the Mediterranean (ix. 10). In the formation of it, every land whither Jews have been banished will restore them. Jehovah declares that he will use His people as bow and arrows against any that would detain them, 'for I have bent Judah for me, I have filled the bow with Ephraim; and I will stir up thy sons, O Zion, against thy sons, O Greece, and will make thee (i.e. Zion) as the sword of a mighty man.' Dr Barnes's paraphrase is that His 'arrows will overtake the slave-dealing Greeks of the Mediterranean, and even from beyond the sea he will deliver his exiles' (p. xvii.). He adds that the words are 'more reasonably ascribed to a writer of the sixth or fifth than to one of the fourth or second century.' Some have suggested that the words in question are an early gloss inserted in the passage, but this is almost too simple a way of solving a difficulty.

(*d*) *The evidence accords with the later part of the fifth century.*

We cannot follow Dr Barnes in making the author an actual 'disciple' of Zechariah. Indeed, the new apocalyptic element (see § 4) marks quite a different line of thought. The prophecy does not seem to be later than the arrival of Nehemiah in Jerusalem in 444, and the book of Malachi, which probably dates from about the same time. How much earlier it was spoken, it is impossible to say. It must be remembered that it is quite likely that Ezra's coming from Babylon and his work at Jerusalem was *after* that of Nehemiah. (See *Ezra and Nehemiah* in this series, p. xxi.) We know nothing whatever of the history of the Jews and their capital during the earlier half of the fifth century. If we may connect these chapters with this obscure period, it adds to their interest and importance. Two facts stand out at the beginning and ending of this unknown period of some seventy years. (i) In 520 Haggai and Zechariah led the people to the highest expectations with regard to the house of David, now restored in the person of Zerubbabel. Not another word is heard about him or his successors. In Zech. ix.–xiv. the house of David reappears amid the promises of a new age, but it is in need of a fountain for its sin and uncleanness. And in spite of these promises, the nation's subsequent destiny is controlled by religious rulers, in the person of the high-priest, and the house of David disappears from view. (ii) The bad news which brought Nehemiah on his mission to Jerusalem was that the returned exiles were 'in great affliction and reproach ; the wall of Jerusalem also is broken down, and the gates thereof are burned with fire' (Neh. i. 3). This cannot refer to 586, but to some recent attempts to fortify the city, which had proved a failure, doubtless owing to a determined attack by those nations round who from the beginning had vigorously objected to the policy of those who rebuilt the temple (see Ezr. iv. and v.). In order to break down the wall and burn the gates, it would be necessary for them to seize the city. In ix.–xiv. we find many references to a capture of Jerusalem by its enemies, and a promise that this shall not happen again. It is possible therefore that this refers, not to 586, but to a recent capture such as is hinted at in Neh. i. 3.

Placing these two things together, we are led to look for further indications in these prophecies both of the serious failure of the civil rulers of the royal house, and of assaults by neighbours all around them, which cruelly frustrated their efforts to fortify the city. Such indications are by no means wanting. (i) The community is ruled over by selfish and tyrannical 'shepherds,' three of whom succeed each other in rapid succession (xi. 5, 16), and a fourth proves still worse, for he involves the community in his ruin (xi. 16, 17, xiii. 7-9). If these were successors of Zerubbabel, this accounts for the silence of the O.T. about the restoration of the house of David after the exile, and also for the hierarchical rule of later times, which preferred the descendants of the high-priest Joshua to those of his royal colleague Zerubbabel. (ii) The theme of xii., xiii. 1-6 and xiv. is a different one. It *may* mean a change of authorship, but more likely only of circumstances. These chapters deal with a cruel attack on the city, which is besieged and captured (xii. 2, xiv. 2), but the tables are soon turned (xii. 2, 4, xiv. 3), and the men of Judah, who appear to have ranged themselves on the enemy's side at first (xii. 2, 5), become the saviours of the city, and receive the first share of glory for it (xii. 6, 7). The prophet need not necessarily be actually pointing back to this, since his language deals with the future, but he may have been largely influenced by it. In these last chapters the enemies are regarded as coming from all quarters, but in chs. ix.-xi. the Philistines are specially mentioned and the peoples of the Phoenician coast and of Syria. This mixed array of hostile neighbours tallies with what is told by Nehemiah, whose chief enemies were Sanballat the Horonite (who seems to have come from within their own borders), Tobiah the Ammonite, and Geshem the Arabian (Neh. ii. 19). In ch. xi. the brotherhood between Judah and Israel is broken (xi. 14), and it was such dissensions among the Jews which Nehemiah shews to have been one of the causes of their weakness. This spirit of quarrelling and disloyalty extended even to the men of Judah, whose nobles (cf. the chieftains of Judah in Zech. xii. 6) actually were in sympathy with the enemies of Nehemiah (Neh. vi. 17, 18). This seems to have been the case in the time of the prophet (see above, and xii. 2, 4).

One more link may be suggested between this prophecy and the work of Nehemiah. In Neh. viii. 16 ff. we are told of a great and universal keeping of the feast of Tabernacles, on an unprecedented scale. This is exactly the climax of the last chapter of Zechariah (xiv. 16 ff.), where it is predicted that all the world will go up to Jerusalem 'to keep the feast of tabernacles.' The existence of this prophecy, and its representation of this great feast as a prelude to a glorious future, may have suggested the keeping of it with 'very great gladness,' as recorded in Neh. viii. 17.

This section must not be made unduly long, but it is perhaps sufficient to suggest the conclusion that the chapters date from just before Nehemiah's coming. And if we ask, whether all these prophecies were falsified, or if there is any sense in which they came true, we may recognise in the magnificent and patriotic success of Nehemiah in restoring Jerusalem to something of its old strength and greatness, the fulfilment of the blessings which the prophet had promised. They came through more human means than he had predicted, but this is the constant method of God's working.

This view will be further illustrated in the notes, but will be kept in the background. But the chief intention is to put the facts and some of the suggested interpretations of them before the readers, and then ask them to make a choice for themselves.

§ 4. THE APOCALYPTIC ELEMENT IN THESE CHAPTERS.

In the last few centuries before the Christian era, a new form of literature arose among the Jews, consisting of apocalypses or 'revelations' of the miraculous interposition of God on behalf of His people. The Book of Revelation is a Christian sequel to them, and the Book of Daniel is an early example. But 'apocalyptic' appeared as a tendency long before it became the sole element in certain

Jewish writings. This tendency is clearly seen in these chapters, and is quite distinct from the visions of Zechariah himself. In his case, Jehovah's blessings were to come by natural means, such as fruitful seasons and political advantage among the nations, and these blessings would depend on the moral behaviour of His people. In 'apocalyptic' there is no moral or human element, but mere marvels whereby God works wondrously for His people, and ruthlessly destroys their enemies. This element is discernible in the language of chs. ix.–xiv. Again apocalyptic pays no heed to the present effect of the revelations, and this is seen in such passages as the one where the capture of Jerusalem itself is predicted, quite apart from warnings concerning sin and repentance (xiv. 1). There is a lack of proportion in apocalyptic which describes things on a huge scale. This is the case in the gathering of the whole earth against Jerusalem (xii. 4 and xiv. 2). It will be seen that these facts not only give interest to these chapters, but also are against the authorship of Zechariah or of any writer of an earlier time.

§ 5. SUMMARY OF CHS. IX.–XIV.

1. The Revival of the Nation.

    (a) The Messianic kingdom established (ix. 1–10).

    (b) The nation restored from all quarters (11–17).

    (c) The oppressors of Israel and Judah overthrown (x. 1–xi. 3).

    (d) The good shepherd and the bad ones (xi. 4–17 and xiii. 7–9).

2. The future of Judah and Jerusalem.

    (a) The deliverance of Jerusalem from the heathen world, and the day of national repentance (xii. 1–xiii. 6).

    (b) Jerusalem, at length delivered from her enemies, is made the centre of the world's worship of Jehovah (xiv.).

I. The Revival of the Nation.

(*a*) ix. 1–10. *The Messianic kingdom established.*

The burden of the word of the LORD upon the land of **9**
Hadrach, and Damascus *shall be* its resting place : for the
eye of man and of all the tribes of Israel is toward the
LORD : and Hamath also which bordereth thereon : Tyre **2**
and Zidon, because she is very wise. And Tyre did build **3**

---

ix. 1–8. The first stage of the new era is marked by the overthrow of the traditional opponents of the nation along the coast-
line of the Mediterranean. Although at various times the Hebrews
had laid claim to a much larger tract than their own country, they
never succeeded in holding it, and there were many nations round
about them who always remained a thorn in their side. The
prophet sees these finally overthrown, while those who remain
after the slaughter come and join themselves to the Jehovah-wor-
shippers of Jerusalem.

1. The burden of the word of *Jehovah.* Prefer the marginal
translation 'oracle.' This first 'utterance' extends for three
chapters. The expression recurs in xii. 1, and also in Mal. i. 1
(see Introd. p. 79), and the actual word often introduces a prophecy, but is not elsewhere used as part of it, e.g. Is. xiii. 1, 'the
burden of (i.e. concerning) Babylon.'

Hadrach: not mentioned elsewhere, but probably to be identified with Hattarika, which is mentioned in Assyrian inscriptions,
and is in Syria.

and Damascus shall be its resting place: i.e. the ancient
capital of Syria shall be a resting place for the word of God's
punishment. But a word must be supplied, and it may be (as
Dr Barnes) 'and against him whose resting place is Damascus,'
i.e. the inhabitants of that city, unprepared for an attack.

for the eye of man, etc. If this rendering is taken, it means
that Jehovah's people were looking to Him to take vengeance.
If, as in R.V. marg., it is 'The LORD hath an eye upon men,' it
means that He is watching them with a view to requital.

2. Hamath also: a city frequently mentioned in the O.T. and
in inscriptions. Although some way north of Damascus (on which
it is here said to 'border') it was claimed as the boundary of
Israel both in Solomon's reign (1 Kings viii. 65) and in that of
Jeroboam II (2 Kings xiv. 25).

Tyre and Zidon: the two great Phoenician cities on the coast.
Tyre was at this time the more important, so that the next clause
because, etc., must refer to her. (Unless with the Septuagint we
read 'they are' for **she is.**)

3. In order to make the city impregnable, a new Tyre was

herself a strong hold, and heaped up silver as the dust, and
4 fine gold as the mire of the streets. Behold, the Lord will
dispossess her, and he will smite her power in the sea ;
5 and she shall be devoured with fire. Ashkelon shall see it,
and fear ; Gaza also, and shall be sore pained ; and Ekron,
for her expectation shall be ashamed : and the king shall
perish from Gaza, and Ashkelon shall not be inhabited.
6 And a bastard shall dwell in Ashdod, and I will cut off the
7 pride of the Philistines. And I will take away his blood
out of his mouth, and his abominations from between his
teeth ; and he also shall be a remnant for our God : and
he shall be as a chieftain in Judah, and Ekron as a Jebusite.

---

built on an island close to the shore of which the fortifications
resisted all attacks until Alexander and his Greeks took them in
332. This verse cannot have been written *after* that event,
for it only anticipates a future overthrow, as does Amos in i. 9–10.

4. he will smite her power in the sea. The commerce of Tyre
made her enormously rich; some day her wealth was to be flung
into the sea. But the R.V. marg. suggests a different thought.
If Jehovah should smite 'the sea which is her rampart,' it looks
forward to the Greeks driving off the seas that sea-borne commerce which was the secret of her greatness.

5. Ashkelon…Gaza…Ekron. The divine punishment upon the
cities sweeps from north to south, and visits the cities of the
Philistines, which would be reached next by a conqueror advanc-
ing along the plains near the sea. Ashdod is mentioned in the
next verse, but the fifth Philistine city, Gath, is passed over, as
in Amos i. 6–8. The whole passage, Amos i. 3–10, should be
compared with this one.

7. his blood out of his mouth, etc. The Jews were of course
forbidden to eat the blood with their meat, and therefore looked
with horror on those who did so. The prophet is doubtless thinking of their heathen sacrifices (as in Ezek. xxxiii. 25), and the
abominations are the animals they would offer, which were
among those regarded by the Jews as unclean.

a remnant for our God. As the returned Jews were themselves
a remnant left after divine punishment, so there should be a
humbled remnant among their foes, who should seek God.

as a chieftain in Judah. The word for chieftain is the one
which occurs so often as 'duke' in Gen. xxxvi. 15–19. But many
editors read 'as a clan,' which gives a more natural sense.

Ekron as a Jebusite : i.e. the inhabitants of Ekron shall be-

And I will encamp about mine house against the army, 8
that none pass through or return : and no oppressor shall
pass through them any more : for now have I seen with
mine eyes.

Rejoice greatly, O daughter of Zion ; shout, O daughter 9
of Jerusalem : behold, thy king cometh unto thee : he is
just, and having salvation ; lowly, and riding upon an ass,

---

come as those of Jebus, who were absorbed in the new population
when David took it and made it into Jerusalem.

8. The mention of Jebus suggests that the holy city shall have
a very different treatment from the hostile cities just mentioned,
for God will defend her.

I will encamp about mine house against the army. If **mine
house** is the temple, it must have been standing then. But it
may mean the holy land, as in Jer. xii. 7, etc. The R.V. marg.
' as a garrison ' is better.

that none pass through or return. The position of Palestine
between Egypt and the empires of the north always meant that
it was subject to being overrun (like Belgium) by armies advanc-
ing and returning from an attack. This was the case centuries
before the rival generals who succeeded to Alexander's empire
traversed it thus.

9-10. The next stage of the new era is the entry of a Prince of
Peace into the holy city, who is the very opposite of the 'oppressor' (or 'exactor' R.V. marg.) of *v.* 8, and will begin a peaceful
reign over all the nations which have been mentioned. The promise
is an echo of earlier prophecy, particularly that of Isaiah (ix. 1-7
and xi. 1-5). Its special interest lies in its quotation in Matth.
xxi. 5, as fulfilled by our Lord's triumphal entry into Jerusalem.

9. O daughter, etc. : this is a personification of the population,
familiar in the prophets.

just, and having salvation. Cf. Is. xi. 4, 'with righteousness
shall he judge the poor.' The second epithet does not seem to
mean that he brings salvation, but that he has received it from
Jehovah, and is thus 'saved' (R.V. marg.), i.e. delivered or
vindicated.

lowly, etc. He is the opposite of an ordinary monarch in his
pomp, and instead of a war-horse he rides the ass, the beast of
peace, like the 'lawgiver' of Gen. xlix. 11, who should bind 'his
ass's colt unto the choice vine.'

even upon a colt. Of course the repetition is simply due to the
poetic form of the clause. There is no suggestion of there being
two animals. St Matthew quotes from the Septuagint, which has
'and' for 'even.'

10 even upon a colt the foal of an ass. And I will cut off the
chariot from Ephraim, and the horse from Jerusalem, and
the battle bow shall be cut off; and he shall speak peace
unto the nations: and his dominion shall be from sea to
sea, and from the River to the ends of the earth.

(*b*) ix. 11–17. *The Nation restored from all quarters.*

11 As for thee also, because of the blood of thy covenant
I have sent forth thy prisoners out of the pit wherein is no
12 water. Turn you to the strong hold, ye prisoners of hope:
even to-day do I declare that I will render double unto
13 thee. For I have bent Judah for me, I have filled the bow

---

10. The rule of the ideal king involves (i) the abolishing of all
instruments of war, (ii) the maintenance of peace, not by force of
arms but by just decrees (**he shall speak peace**), (iii) an empire
as wide as the earth.

from sea to sea, etc. The same words describe the dominions
of the ideal king in Ps. lxxii. 8. One sea is of course the Mediterranean, the other should be eastwards rather than the Red Sea,
'the vaguely known sea supposed to encircle the E. of Asia'
(Driver). The River is of course the Euphrates; the whole recalls
the borders of Solomon's empire.

11–12. The exiles, returned from their tribulations to their own
city, may hope for twice as much of joy as they have had of sorrow.

11. As for thee also...I have sent forth. Jerusalem is again
addressed, as in *v.* 9. It is better rendered 'Thou, thou also hast
sent forth.'

because of the blood: probably referring to the original covenant of Exod. xxiv. 5-8, and not their blood shed for the sake
of the covenant.

12. the strong hold. The reference is doubtful, but it seems
to be Zion. However, it may be Jehovah Himself to Whom they
are to turn in fresh confidence.

ye prisoners of hope: i.e. exiles who still expect release, in spite
of their sufferings in dungeons where they cannot quench their
thirst.

13–16. God will use His people to win the victory over the
nations, which will herald the new age, and bring peace and plenty.

13. I have filled the bow with Ephraim: i.e. as His arrows,
or 'drawn out Ephraim as a bow,' i.e. Jehovah will use both the
southern and the northern kingdom as His instrument. The
two, so long apart, will be united by being used as His bow.

with Ephraim; and I will stir up thy sons, O Zion, against
thy sons, O Greece, and will make thee as the sword of a
mighty man. And the LORD shall be seen over them, and 14
his arrow shall go forth as the lightning: and the Lord
GOD shall blow the trumpet, and shall go with whirlwinds
of the south. The LORD of hosts shall defend them; and 15
they shall devour, and shall tread down the sling stones;
and they shall drink, and make a noise as through wine:
and they shall be filled like bowls, like the corners of the
altar. And the LORD their God shall save them in that 16
day as the flock of his people: for *they shall be as* the
stones of a crown, lifted on high over his land. For how 17
great is his goodness, and how great is his beauty! corn

For the questions of date raised by 'Ephraim' and 'Greece,'
see Introd. pp. 78 and 81.

I will stir up thy sons, etc. The men of Jerusalem will be as
arrows in God's hands, and will be directed against those from
the far west who had so often acted as the pirates of the Mediterranean and kidnapped members of their nation. For note on
Javan (Greece), see Introd. pp. 81 and 82; also for the possibility that part of the clause is a gloss.

14. shall be seen over them: hovering in visible form for
their defence.

shall blow the trumpet: i.e. shall give the signal for battle.

15. they shall devour, etc. Either 'they shall devour their
enemies, and trample the sling-stones hurled against them,' or
'the sling-stones (i.e. Jehovah's hail-stones) shall devour and tread
down the enemy.'

they shall be filled like bowls: i.e. they shall be filled with
the blood of their enemies, as full as the bowls of sacrificial blood,
which is dashed against the sides of the altar.

16. This verse gives a startling transition from blood to beauty.
The elaborate simile compares them to the jewels of the holy city,
which is Jehovah's crown, and His ensign seen from afar. But if
we read, as R.V. marg., 'glittering upon his land,' the comparison may still be to a flock of sheep 'glittering under the oriental
sun' (Mitchell).

17. his goodness...his beauty. It seems as if one ought to
refer to Jehovah and the other to His people. The R.V. marg., by
translating the first as 'prosperity,' and substituting 'their' for
'his' in both cases, makes the whole sentence refer to the happy
condition of the restored community. The corn and wine are two

shall make the young men flourish, and new wine the maids.

(c) x. 1–xi. 3. *The oppressors of Israel and Judah overthrown.*

10   Ask ye of the LORD rain in the time of the latter rain, *even of* the LORD that maketh lightnings; and he shall give them showers of rain, to every one grass in the field.
2 For the teraphim have spoken vanity, and the diviners have seen a lie; and they have told false dreams, they comfort in vain: therefore they go their way like sheep, 3 they are afflicted, because there is no shepherd. Mine

---

chief products of the land; their abundance will bring an increase of the population. There is of course no suggestion in the Hebrew verse that one product is for the young men and the other for the maids.

x. 1–2. These verses form a transition from one theme to the next. The abundant harvests of ix. 17 suggest the need to pray to God for the rain to come at the time it is needed and expected. And the sad fact that the people have sought rain through mere superstitious practices, wandering like sheep without a true shepherd to lead them, suggests the false shepherds of *v.* 3 which introduce the next paragraph.

1. the latter rain: i.e. the spring rain, needed a little while before the harvest.

that maketh lightnings: these being the accompaniments of rain. It is a rare word, and may mean 'clouds' (as A.V.), the next clause declaring that God works through natural means, by giving to the *clouds* showers of rain.

2. teraphim: or 'idols,' as A.V. From Ezek. xxi. 21 we learn that these 'images' were 'consulted' in order to arrive at decisions. In early days the use of them was not condemned. Laban's teraphim seem to be of the nature of household gods (Gen. xxxi. 19), and there is nothing in the narrative of 1 Sam. xix. 13 to imply that it was considered wrong for David to possess them.

diviners...dreams. The history of Joseph is connected with both; he had a cup for divining, and his dreams proved the salvation of Egypt. But the prophets denounced those who claimed falsely to have used such means for prophesying (e.g. Jer. xxiii. 25 and xxvii. 9).

they go their way like sheep: i.e. wander about without any fixed aim, because of such sham guidance.

anger is kindled against the shepherds, and I will punish
the he-goats: for the LORD of hosts hath visited his flock
the house of Judah, and shall make them as his goodly
horse in the battle. From him shall come forth the corner 4
stone, from him the nail, from him the battle bow, from
him every exactor together. And they shall be as mighty 5
men, treading down *their enemies* in the mire of the streets
in the battle; and they shall fight, because the LORD is
with them: and the riders on horses shall be confounded.
And I will strengthen the house of Judah, and I will save 6
the house of Joseph, and I will bring them again, for I have
mercy upon them; and they shall be as though I had not
cast them off: for I am the LORD their God, and I will
hear them. And *they of* Ephraim shall be like a mighty 7
man, and their heart shall rejoice as through wine: yea,
their children shall see it, and rejoice; their heart shall be
glad in the LORD. I will hiss for them, and gather them; 8
for I have redeemed them: and they shall increase as they
have increased. And I will sow them among the peoples; 9

---

3. shepherds...he-goats. These are evidently rulers, but it is
not certain whether their own bad rulers, which would include
prophets and priests, are meant. The fighting in *v.* 5 points
rather to their being foreign leaders who have oppressed Judah.

4. This verse declares that all Judah's true leaders are sent by
God. The names are fanciful ones. **Corner stone** suggests 'com-
mander-in-chief'; **nail**, a leader of a household, on whom the
rest depend (cf. Is. xxii. 23 ff.), or 'tent-pin,' which is their support; **battle bow**, the mainstay of the army; and **exactor**, the
man who exacts from them their military service.

5. in the mire: or 'as the mire,' as in Ps. xviii. 42.

6. I will save the house of Joseph. The important tribe of
Ephraim (son of Joseph) stands for the whole of the ten tribes of
the Northern kingdom. Cf. *v.* 7. They are promised a return
from exile, and a share in the new kingdom.

8. I will hiss for them: i.e. call them together, by whistling
as a shepherd to his flock, or perhaps (as Driver) a metaphor
from calling bees.

as they have increased: i.e. as they have in time past. This
promise suggests that the words in *v.* 7 should be rendered 'yea,
they shall see their children.'

9. I will sow them among the peoples: i.e. there shall be a

and they shall remember me in far countries: and they
10 shall live with their children, and shall return. I will bring
them again also out of the land of Egypt, and gather them
out of Assyria; and I will bring them into the land of
Gilead and Lebanon; and *place* shall not be found for
11 them. And he shall pass through the sea of affliction, and
shall smite the waves in the sea, and all the depths of the
Nile shall dry up: and the pride of Assyria shall be brought
12 down, and the sceptre of Egypt shall depart away. And
I will strengthen them in the LORD; and they shall walk
up and down in his name, saith the LORD.

---

new dispersion, not for adversity, but for increase. But R.V.
marg. suggests another sense. If a slight change is made, and the
verb put in the past tense, the reference is to the original dispersion, viz. 'though I scattered them among the peoples.' Van
Hoonacker places *v.* 9 before *v.* 8, as first in logical sequence.

10. Egypt...Assyria. There is no need to take their presence
in Egypt as referring to the period of Greek domination. Egypt
was the original 'house of bondage'; and also in the days of
Pharaoh Necoh many were doubtless taken captive thither (see
2 Kings xxiii. 29, 34).

'Assyria' in any case stands for the country formerly occupied
by the Assyrian empire, but afterwards by the powers that succeeded it. The name has a natural connexion with Ephraim,
as having caused their exile.

Gilead and Lebanon. These localities represent the E. and W.
parts of the Northern kingdom, perhaps because they were among
the glories of the land (see Jer. xxii. 6).

11. he shall pass through the sea, etc. Either the subject is
Jehovah, who will lead His people through all obstacles, as He
led them through the Red Sea; or it is still the people who shall
pass safely through all the rivers that hinder their return. Van
Hoonacker follows the Septuagint, and reads 'they shall pass.'

the sea of affliction: lit. 'the sea-straitness.' The miracle of
the Red Sea is pictured as repeated elsewhere, the waters mentioned before 'the depths of the Nile' probably being those of the
Euphrates.

the sceptre of Egypt: lit. 'the rod,' i.e. the cruelty with which
their traditional history had always associated Egyptian bondage
(see note on *v.* 10).

12. they shall walk up and down in his name: i.e. they
shall live their lives as His servants. Van Hoonacker, who places
x. 3–12 after xi., considers this verse to be a summing up of the

Open thy doors, O Lebanon, that the fire may devour **11**
thy cedars. Howl, O fir tree, for the cedar is fallen, because **2**
the goodly ones are spoiled : howl, O ye oaks of Bashan,
for the strong forest is come down. A voice of the howling **3**
of the shepherds! for their glory is spoiled: a voice of the
roaring of young lions! for the pride of Jordan is spoiled.

(*d*) xi. 4–17 and xiii. 7–9. *The good Shepherd, and
the bad ones.*

Thus said the LORD my God : Feed the flock of **4**

---

prophecies contained in ix.–xi. In Driver's arrangement of four
authors for these six chapters, the work of the first ends after ch. x.
In our own arrangement of subjects, the new topic begins with
the shepherds in xi. 3, the first two verses of xi. still referring to
the overthrow of oppressors.

xi. 1-3. Many commentators take these verses as introducing
the 'shepherds' or bad rulers denounced in the verses which
follow. But they also seem to carry on the thought of the overthrow of oppressors contained in x. 3–12, where the word 'shepherds' was used in *v.* 3. In any case the language is figurative.
Either the 'shepherds' are the rulers of Judah, who 'howl' because the land is laid waste; or else they are the foreign oppressors, whose advance will lead them through the various
forests, and cause the lions to roar which are disturbed by their
armies.

2. for the cedar is fallen : and therefore their turn would
come next.

oaks of Bashan. There was a forest on the mountain slopes
east of Jordan, in regions which were 'strong' and inaccessible.

3. the pride of Jordan is spoiled : i.e. the narrow strip of
luxuriant land along the banks is laid waste.

4-14. An ideal pastor here stands in contrast with those wicked
rulers of the people, who only make a gain of the flock. The
speaker himself, as representing Jehovah, assumes the rôle of the
prophet-shepherd. Van Hoonacker (*op. cit.* p. 671) says that this
rôle must be realised as one of justice rather than of goodness, if
we would grasp the meaning of the allegory, wherein the two
staves are broken for the wrongs that have been done. The
reference is to a past age. The people's rejection of Jehovah in the
last days of the monarchy was shewn by their treatment of Jeremiah, the prophet who represented Him then. Not only did
Zedekiah 'humble not himself before Jeremiah the prophet speaking from the mouth of Jehovah' (2 Chron. xxxvi. 12), but the
prophet was submitted to all kinds of cruelties and indignities.

5 slaughter ; whose possessors slay them, and hold themselves not guilty; and they that sell them say, Blessed be
the LORD, for I am rich : and their own shepherds pity
6 them not. For I will no more pity the inhabitants of the
land, saith the LORD : but, lo, I will deliver the men every
one into his neighbour's hand, and into the hand of his
king : and they shall smite the land, and out of their hand
7 I will not deliver them. So I fed the flock of slaughter,
verily the poor of the flock. And I took unto me two

---

vv. 11–14 may therefore refer to Jeremiah, when, in Jehovah's
place, he was treated as a slave, whose value was 30 pieces of silver
(Jer. xlii. 1–xliii. 7). In this case it is he who makes indignant
protest. The people are now reminded of this, because they are
treating Jehovah in the same way again.

To ourselves, though not to the prophet, is suggested the picture of the Good Shepherd who cares for the sheep, and yet is
scorned and rejected, in contrast with the hireling shepherds who
care nothing.

But many other theories have been suggested by the 'three
shepherds' of *v.* 8, who are claimed by some as pointing to the
Greek period. See note on the verse, where the view of the
present writer is expressed.

4 Feed the flock of slaughter. The first words imply a
shepherd who cares for the flock, for the verb is in the singular.
The words **of slaughter** may best be explained by *v.* 5, as the
flock which are being destroyed by their present shepherds. But
Mitchell, who takes the shepherd as meaning not God but a king,
explains that 'the sheep are being prepared for the shambles.'

5. The statement that the people are sold as well as bought
by their present rulers points to the rendering 'buyers' of R.V.
marg., rather than **possessors.** The verse implies that miscarriage
of justice which the Hebrew prophets had to denounce so often.

Blessed be the Lord, etc. The shepherds veil their extortions
under a cloak of piety.

their own shepherds pity them not. It will be seen from *v.* 6
that **pity** has the active sense of rescue. This makes probable
the rendering of the R.V. marg. 'their shepherd pitieth them
not.' This either means Jehovah, as represented by His prophet-
shepherd, who does not come to the rescue; or their king in the
last days of the monarchy, who was as bad as those who ruled
under him. The opening words of *v.* 6, **For I will no more pity**,
favour the former interpretation.

7. the poor of the flock. But the whole of the sorry flock is

staves; the one I called Beauty, and the other I called
Bands; and I fed the flock. And I cut off the three 8
shepherds in one month; for my soul was weary of them,

---

meant, so prefer as R.V. marg. 'the most miserable of sheep.'
Their feeding is in obedience to the command of v. 4.

two staves...Beauty, and...Bands. The oriental shepherd
carried two sticks, a short rod or club, to drive off wild beasts,
etc., and a longer staff to lean on and use for guiding the flock.
Cf. Ps. xxiii. 4, 'Thy rod and thy staff comfort me.' So the
action is a natural one, but the names are symbolic. **Beauty,**
which should be rendered as R.V. marg. 'Graciousness,' is explained in v. 10 (see note) as Jehovah's covenant which He severs.
Bands, or rather 'Binders' or 'Union,' stands in v. 14 for the
brotherhood which binds the tribes together. Thus by their own
folly they forfeit the two relationships which are the secrets of
their defence, the fatherhood of God and the brotherhood of man.
Dr Barnes refers the words to Jeremiah's time, when God tried
in vain to help His people by two means, the Priesthood, and
the House of David.

8. the three shepherds in one month. This verse has been an
important factor in the attempts to find a date for the prophecy. See
Introd. pp. 79 and 84. If it is a historical allusion, it may mean:
(i) Three of the last kings of Israel, who were cut off one after the
other, as the nation hastened to its fall. (ii) Three kings of Judah,
just before its fall: either Jehoiakim, Jehoiachin, and Zedekiah,
whose rule brought punishment in the destruction of Jerusalem in
586 by the Babylonians, or (as Van Hoonacker, *op. cit.* p. 675) the
three mentioned in Jer. xxii. 9 ff., Jehoahaz (Shallum), Jehoiakim,
and Jehoiachin (Jeconiah). This explanation agrees with the iden-
tification of the prophet-shepherd with Jeremiah. (iii) The three
offices of king, priest, and prophet, supposed to be brought to an end
in that same year. (iv) An allusion to the Greek period, the three
perhaps being the empires of Assyria, Babylonia, and Persia.
(v) A prediction of the fall of Antiochus Epiphanes (164 B.C.)
and his two successors who reigned over Syria. (vi) Three high-
priests of the Maccabaean period, from which time some would
date the verse. (Mitchell regards it as a gloss, by one 'who
thought he saw in the parable a time when three rulers, one after
another in rapid succession, were removed.') Kirkpatrick (*op.
cit.* p. 463), on the other hand, regards the three shepherds as
simply 'a part of the furniture of the allegory,' and therefore not
to be sought for in history. The present writer's suggestion (see
Introd. p. 84) is that Zerubbabel, who had himself disappointed
the expectations of the prophets in 520, was succeeded by three
worthless rulers of the house of David, whose rule proved so

9 and their soul also loathed me. Then said I, I will not
feed you: that that dieth, let it die; and that that is to be
cut off, let it be cut off; and let them which are left eat
10 every one the flesh of another. And I took my staff Beauty,
and cut it asunder, that I might break my covenant which
11 I had made with all the peoples. And it was broken in
that day; and thus the poor of the flock that gave heed
12 unto me knew that it was the word of the LORD. And I
said unto them, If ye think good, give me my hire; and
if not, forbear. So they weighed for my hire thirty *pieces*
13 of silver. And the LORD said unto me, Cast it unto the
potter, the goodly price that I was prised at of them. And
I took the thirty *pieces* of silver, and cast them unto the

---

disastrous for the restored community that Jerusalem was in the
sorry plight wherein it was found by Nehemiah in 444.

9. Then said I: viz., Jehovah, who gives up the attempt to
shepherd His heedless sheep.

10. my covenant which I had made with all the peoples.
At first sight this seems to mean peace with the nations outside,
and some refer it to their relations with the neighbouring peoples,
such as Edomites, Philistines, and Samaritans, who proved such
a continual source of trouble. But as the word for **peoples** is not
the one used for Gentiles, it may be the various tribes who are
intended. This suits better with the fact that the covenant is
Jehovah's own. The staff Graciousness is then explained as standing for all the institutions which God had given to Judah, including
the priesthood and temple.

12. The prophet-shepherd now demands his wages, in reward
for the office in which he represents Jehovah. Both are insulted
by the offer of a paltry sum which, in the code of Exod. xxi. 32, is
the price paid for injury to a slave. It represents about £4 of our
money.

13. Cast it unto the potter. This is a sarcasm, suggesting that
the sum might pay for the hire of a craftsman for making cheap
vessels, but not for God's work. For the alternative reading, see
the next note.

cast them unto the potter, in the house of the Lord. The
action of protest is appropriately made by the prophet in the pre-
cincts of the temple itself. But great difficulty has been found in
the words, both in ancient and modern times. Van Hoonacker
suggests that the original was 'in *his* house,' i.e. the potter's
(l'atelier du potier, *op. cit.* p. 677), and is in imitation of Jer.

potter, in the house of the LORD. Then I cut asunder 14
mine other staff, even Bands, that I might break the
brotherhood between Judah and Israel.

And the LORD said unto me, Take unto thee yet again 15

---

xviii. 2 ff. (*q.v.*). But there is a doubt whether the 'potter' was
originally mentioned at all in either part of the verse. A slight
change gives the reading of the Syriac version (followed by the
R.V. marg. in both places), viz. 'into the treasury,' instead of
'unto the potter.' The prophet is in this case bidden to offer the
sum by way of protest for the use of God's house, which the returned Jews were so apt to neglect.

The verse is famous for the quotation of it in Matth. xxvii. 9, as
fulfilled in the buying of the potter's field with the blood-money
returned by Judas. It is to be noted: (i) That the Evangelist
ascribes the words to Jeremiah, perhaps through its likeness to
Jer. xviii. mentioned above. (For the theory which ascribes these
chapters to that prophet, see Introd. p. 79.) (ii) That his quotation differs widely from any known text, ending 'and gave them
for the potter's field, as the Lord appointed me.' But it is remarkable that 'the treasury' is at least hinted at in *v.* 5, when
Judas 'cast down the pieces of silver in the temple' (or 'threw
them into the sanctuary'). This is one of the many places where
the language of the O.T. suggests itself to a N.T. writer, though
the thought of the latter may not have been present in the original.
If an inner meaning is to be sought in the 'potter,' it is the lesson
of the visit to the potter's house in Jer. xviii., viz. that the divine
Potter has power to treat His people as clay, and will mar them in
His hand if they do not return to Him. This may be said to lead
to the action of *v.* 14.

•14. The breaking of the first staff in *v.* 10 has severed them from
Jehovah's covenant; the breaking of the second symbolizes the loss
of brotherhood between them. The mention of Israel along with
Judah is of course remarkable, but it cannot be said to point to
an early date, for before the exile no brotherhood existed between
them. If we are right in ascribing the prophecy to the dark years
before Nehemiah's coming, there may have been an understand-
ing for a while between Jerusalem and the Jews living further
north, which came to an abrupt ending, and further embarrassed
the position of the city, which was already surrounded with
enemies, whose action seems to have led to the reproach that
'the wall of Jerusalem also is broken down, and the gates thereof
are burned with fire' (Neh. i. 3). See Introd. p. 83.

15–17. So far the prophet has impersonated the divine Shepherd. But now that the rejection has taken place, he is bidden
to punish the flock by assuming a new rôle, and representing a

16 the instruments of a foolish shepherd. For, lo, I will raise
up a shepherd in the land, which shall not visit those that
be cut off, neither shall seek those that be scattered, nor
heal that that is broken; neither shall he feed that which
is sound, but he shall eat the flesh of the fat, and shall
17 tear their hoofs in pieces. Woe to the worthless shepherd
that leaveth the flock! the sword shall be upon his arm,
and upon his right eye: his arm shall be clean dried up,
and his right eye shall be utterly darkened.

'foolish shepherd,' who, after cruel treatment of the flock, shall
himself receive the punishment he deserves for deserting them.
There is little doubt that the sequel of this prophecy is to be
found in xiii. 7–9, which predicts that there will be a terrible
judgment on the flock when the shepherd is smitten by Jehovah's
sword, but that ultimate blessing shall fall upon the purified
remnant.

15. the instruments of a foolish shepherd. A shepherd's
equipment includes, in addition to the rod and staff already mentioned, a 'shepherd's bag' such as that in which David put the five
stones (1 Sam. xvii. 40), and a shepherd's pipe. The epithet
foolish implies sinfulness, as often in the O.T. Driver (*op. cit.*
p. 260) says his instruments must be pictured as 'worn out and
useless.'

16. I will raise up a shepherd. The question again arises as
to whether a historical personage is meant. If the 'three shepherds' are Jehoahaz, Jehoiakim, and Jehoiachin, then this is
Zedekiah, who brought final ruin on his people. Possibly his blind-
ing is referred to in *v.* 17, 'his right eye shall be utterly darkened.'
Some think that, as in xiii. 7 Jehovah calls him 'my fellow,' he
must be a high-priest, which suits late date. Others would recognise in him Ptolemy Philopator. Or, if Zerubbabel had three
unworthy successors, there is no reason why there should not have
been yet another, as they all fell in so short a space of time (*v.* 8).

which shall not visit, etc. The best commentary is to be found
in the reproof of 'the shepherds of Israel that do feed themselves'
in Ezek. xxxiv. There, after telling of their neglect, the prophet
represents God as intervening with 'I, even I, will both search
my sheep, and seek them out' (*v.* 11). The words are like those
of Him who came to seek and to save those that are lost.

shall tear their hoofs in pieces. Either this means that they
will eat up even their hoofs, or that they will over-drive them on
rough ground. Dr Barnes says the word 'hoofs' probably means
'pieces,' and so translates 'shall tear them in pieces.'

17. his arm shall be clean dried up, etc. He shall be punished

II. THE FUTURE OF JUDAH AND JERUSALEM.

(*a*) xii. 1–xiii. 6. *The deliverance of Jerusalem from the heathen world, and the day of national repentance.*

The burden of the word of the LORD concerning Israel. **12**
Thus saith the LORD, which stretcheth forth the heavens, and layeth the foundation of the earth, and formeth the spirit of man within him: Behold, I will make Jerusalem 2 a cup of reeling unto all the peoples round about, and upon

---

by losing the power of those very members which ought to have been active in guarding the flock.

The best way to study this commentary is to proceed at once to xiii. 7–9, and then return afterwards for the prophecy contained in xii. 1–xiii. 6.

xii. 1–xiii. 6. This section is the first part of the prophecy which forms the second half of these six chapters. It is thought by many to be the work of a different author. In the more elaborate partition of the chapters among four authors this section is reckoned as A³, being the work of a third author. (See Introd. p. 80.)

1–9. The first part of this chapter has a subject akin to that of the earlier verses of xiv., viz. the seizure and deliverance of Jerusalem. In both places the prophet dwells at length on the deliverance, in order to comfort his people, while the capture of the holy city is passed over in a single verse (xiii. 2 and xiv. 2). The comfort lies in the overthrow of the nations which attack Jerusalem. This Jehovah Himself will effect, but the people of Judah will be moved to give their aid.

1. The burden of the word, etc. See note on ix. 1. The repetition of this introduction, and its recurrence at the beginning of Malachi (which also appears to be an anonymous prophecy), is one of the arguments for taking this as the work of a different author from ix.–xi., and for thinking that three separate prophecies have been placed by an editor after the work of Zechariah, each being introduced by the same formula.

concerning Israel. This cannot mean Israel as distinct from Judah (as in xi. 14), but must include all the people of the land, as in ix. 1.

which stretcheth forth the heavens, etc. This prophecy of God's power is appropriately introduced by epithets which remind them that He is all-powerful.

2. a cup of reeling. This is an ambiguous phrase. If it be a cup or bowl of reeling, it means that the nations seize Jerusalem to drink it down, and it has the effect of making them stagger with intoxication. In Is. lxi. 22 it is Jehovah Who makes them

3 Judah also shall it be in the siege against Jerusalem. And it shall come to pass in that day, that I will make Jerusalem a burdensome stone for all the peoples; all that burden themselves with it shall be sore wounded; and all the nations of the earth shall be gathered together against it.

4 In that day, saith the LORD, I will smite every horse with astonishment, and his rider with madness: and I will open mine eyes upon the house of Judah, and will smite every

5 horse of the peoples with blindness. And the chieftains of Judah shall say in their heart, The inhabitants of Jerusalem

---

drink it in His anger. But the Hebrew can mean 'threshold' as well as 'bowl.' If it is 'a threshold of trembling' it suggests that the foes of Jerusalem will flee from it as if they thought the threshold was shaking with an earthquake. Such flight is alluded to in xiv. 5. The Septuagint supports this by reading 'a shaking vestibule.'

and upon Judah also, etc. Judah seems to have taken part with the enemies of Jerusalem, but the blow shall fall on them likewise. 'Shall it fall to be' of R.V. marg. means that Judah will have to take part in the siege. But the subsequent blessing on Judah makes this hard to understand. It is better to read (as Van Hoonacker and Barnes) 'upon Judah also shall there be affliction because of Jerusalem.'

3. a burdensome stone: i.e. a stone on which the peoples hurt themselves, as the next clause explains. It may be simply a metaphor from pushing a heavy stone, which hurts the hands of those who do it; or, from the frequency with which masons must in those days have been 'sore wounded' by being crushed with the heavy stones they had to put in place.

all the nations of the earth. This exaggeration is in apocalyptic style. See Introd. p. 86.

4. I will open mine eyes upon the house of Judah: i.e. I will shew favour. If v. 2 means that Judah began by fighting against Jerusalem, they now change their minds. But how can the chief blessing fall, as in v. 7, upon those who for a while had played the traitor to their countrymen? The insistence seems rather on the prominent part taken throughout by those in the country round. If they shared in the affliction, it was fitting that they should have their reward, even taking precedence of the princes and people of Jerusalem.

every horse of the peoples. The Jews always dreaded foreign cavalry, as they had none themselves. Cf. x. 5.

5. the chieftains of Judah. See note on ix. 7.

are my strength in the LORD of hosts their God. In that 6
day will I make the chieftains of Judah like a pan of fire
among wood, and like a torch of fire among sheaves; and
they shall devour all the peoples round about, on the right
hand and on the left: and Jerusalem shall yet again dwell
in her own place, even in Jerusalem. The LORD also shall 7
save the tents of Judah first, that the glory of the house of
David and the glory of the inhabitants of Jerusalem be not
magnified above Judah. In that day shall the LORD defend 8
the inhabitants of Jerusalem; and he that is feeble among
them at that day shall be as David; and the house of
David shall be as God, as the angel of the LORD before
them. And it shall come to pass in that day, that I will 9
seek to destroy all the nations that come against Jerusalem.

---

6. like a pan of fire among wood. The havoc wrought by the
men of Judah is compared to a brazier containing a fire, which
would soon set the wood in a blaze if it came in contact with it.

Jerusalem shall yet again dwell, etc. The city had only been
partially restored, and the walls were not yet built.

7. shall save the tents of Judah first: i.e. the country people
shall be the chief gainers for supporting the capital. Such an
encouragement to them to be loyal to it was doubtless needed,
for they might well refuse to exalt, to their own loss, a city which
invited the attacks of their enemies. The verse hints at quarrels
and parties within and without the capital. One of the difficulties
Nehemiah had to contend with was the reluctance of the population to come to Jerusalem (see Neh. xi. 1, 2), and he records the
disloyalty of the 'nobles of Judah' (vi. 17).

8. The holy city receives far more than human help, and
Jehovah gives them such new strength that even 'he that stum-
bleth' (Heb. and R.V. marg.) will become a warrior like David.
The exalted and spiritualised position of **the house of David**
shews that there was still hope of their revival. But this does not
contradict the suggestion that not only had Zerubbabel disappointed their hopes, but his successors had given them the exact
opposite of divine guidance.

shall be as God. The Hebrew need not mean as much as the
English, but is like that of Gen. iii. 5, where the serpent tells
Adam and Eve 'ye shall be as gods' (R.V. marg.). Otherwise
there is no point in the further comparison to **the angel of the
Lord.** It is not Jehovah's name that is used.

10 And I will pour upon the house of David, and upon the
inhabitants of Jerusalem, the spirit of grace and of supplication ; and they shall look unto me whom they have pierced :
and they shall mourn for him, as one mourneth for his
only son, and shall be in bitterness for him, as one that
11 is in bitterness for his firstborn. In that day shall there
be a great mourning in Jerusalem, as the mourning of

10–14. The deliverance is succeeded by an act of repentance,
and a universal lamentation for some well-known martyr whom
they had rejected and put to death.

10. The entire people, rulers and ruled, will be filled with an
impulse to obtain the grace of forgiveness, and to make supplication for it. They will seek it with bitter wailing.

they shall look unto me whom they have pierced. There is
little doubt that we must follow those Heb. MSS which read
'him.' The only explanation of 'me' is that Jehovah identifies
Himself with His martyr, but the use of the 3rd person in the
rest of the sentence is against this.

The author does not seem to have intended to conceal the
man's name, but to take it for granted that his readers knew it.
Some ruler (Dr Barnes says possibly Zerubbabel himself) has
been put to death, perhaps because his righteous leadership displeased the demoralised community. If the successors of Zerubbabel were wicked 'shepherds,' as has been suggested, this man
may have been the victim of their misrule. And if he were not
himself of the royal line, we can understand why the **house of
David** was to take so prominent a part in the act of lamentation.
Some consider that it was a series of godly men who had been
martyred, but they are spoken of as one, in the same way as the
righteous sufferers are made singular in the 'servant of Jehovah'
who was 'despised and rejected of men' in Is. liii.

The appropriateness of the language in relation to the cruci-
fixion is recognised in John xix. 37, where these words are quoted,
and also in Rev. i. 7.

**11. as the mourning of Hadadrimmon in the valley of Me-
giddon.** This evidently is taken as typical of grief at an over-
whelming loss through death, but the actual reference is very
uncertain. (i) The chief clue lies in the last word, which recalls
the fact that when king Josiah was killed in battle with Pharaoh
Necoh at Megiddo, he was taken to Jerusalem and, at the in-
stigation of Jeremiah, 'all Judah and Jerusalem mourned for
Josiah.' The chronicler adds that the lamentations were continued 'to this day' (2 Chron. xxxv. 22–25). This explanation

Hadadrimmon in the valley of Megiddon. And the land 12
shall mourn, every family apart; the family of the house
of David apart, and their wives apart; the family of the
house of Nathan apart, and their wives apart; the family 13
of the house of Levi apart, and their wives apart; the
family of the Shimeites apart, and their wives apart; all 14
the families that remain, every family apart, and their
wives apart.

---

leaves the word **Hadadrimmon** unexplained, for the statement
(as made by Jerome) that it was a place near Megiddo, where the
mourning was made, seems little more than a guess. (ii) Another
explanation explains 'Hadadrimmon' but not 'Megiddon.' It
may be, not a historical allusion, but a religious custom, modelled
on heathen rites. For in several religions, there is a mourning
for a sorely wounded god, such as Adonis or Tammuz. Ezekiel
speaks of this as one of the corruptions which had reached Jerusalem, for he saw at the temple gate 'women weeping for
Tammuz' (Ezek. viii. 14). The word Hadadrimmon may therefore be the name of a deity, perhaps equivalent to Adonis. We
know of Rimmon as a Syrian god (2 Kings v. 18), and Hadad
appears in such names as Benhadad. As the Septuagint reads
only 'Rimmon,' Van Hoonacker suggests that that was the
original word, and that 'Hadad' was added as a gloss, being the
name of another Syrian deity. He thus favours the second of
the above two explanations. But it seems better to take the one
which depends on the familiar word Megiddo, than that which
is based on the unknown 'Hadadrimmon.'
   the valley: i.e. the plain. Megiddo was on the S.W. of the
wide plain of Esdraelon, where so many battles have been fought,
including Allenby's *coup* in recent years.
   12–14. This universal lamentation is to be fulfilled in an orderly
way; the families form themselves into groups, the sexes being
kept apart. The royal house is put first, and the priestly third in
the list of four. The other two are uncertain. Perhaps they are
each a subdivision of the preceding one, Nathan being the son
of David and Shimei the grandson of Levi, whose family is mentioned in Num. iii. 21. But Nathan may be an abbreviated form,
standing for some high-priestly family, and Shimei may mean the
tribe of Simeon (as given in the Septuagint), which was the
southern tribe traditionally connected with Levi. (See Gen.
xlix. 5.)
   14. all the families that remain: viz. all the other families in
like manner.

13 In that day there shall be a fountain opened to the
house of David and to the inhabitants of Jerusalem, for
2 sin and for uncleanness. And it shall come to pass in that
day, saith the LORD of hosts, that I will cut off the names
of the idols out of the land, and they shall no more be
remembered: and also I will cause the prophets and the
3 unclean spirit to pass out of the land. And it shall come
to pass that, when any shall yet prophesy, then his father
and his mother that begat him shall say unto him, Thou
shalt not live; for thou speakest lies in the name of the
LORD: and his father and his mother that begat him shall

---

xiii. 1–6. Repentance and lamentation are naturally followed
by forgiveness. Their sins will be pardoned, and all corrupting
influences will be removed. These consisted of more than open
idolatry, for the prophets had debased their office and proved
unfaithful to Jehovah. Henceforth such men will be ashamed to
let others know their position.

1. there shall be a fountain opened, etc. Water was regularly
used to wash away ceremonial impurity (here termed **uncleanness**).
Here its use is extended to the cleansing from inward sinfulness.
There is special meaning in the promise that, in the waterless city
of Jerusalem, Jehovah will grant a living spring, which will always
give an abundant supply to all who need it. See note on xiv. 8.

to the house of David, etc. Perhaps the phrase simply means
'for rulers and people alike.' But this special mention of the
royal house and its need of cleansing supports the theory that it
had specially sinned, through its wicked 'shepherds.'

2. the names of the idols: i.e. the power and influence of the
idols, and all that they stood for. The 'name' of Jehovah is often
similarly used, e.g. in Is. xxx. 24.

the prophets and the unclean spirit. Although the Septuagint renders 'false prophets,' it seems probable that all prophecy
had become debased, as it had sometimes in the past (see 1 Kings
xxii. 23 and Jer. v. 31). The 'spirit of uncleanness,' like the
'spirit of supplication' in xii. 10, means the impulse which moved
them.

3. Such a man will have so brought the prophetic office into
disrepute that his parents will prefer to cause his death rather
than that he should bring them such dishonour. In Deut. xiii.
6–10 a man's nearest relations are bidden to kill him if he attempts secretly to lure them away from the worship of Jehovah.

If the reference is to the prophet's own day, we can understand his preferring to remain anonymous.

thrust him through when he prophesieth. And it shall 4
come to pass in that day, that the prophets shall be ashamed
every one of his vision, when he prophesieth ; neither shall
they wear a hairy mantle to deceive : but he shall say, I am 5
no prophet, I am a tiller of the ground ; for I have been
made a bondman from my youth. And one shall say unto 6
him, What are these wounds between thine arms ? Then
he shall answer, Those with which I was wounded in the
house of my friends.

xiii. 7–9. Continuation of the prophecy of xi. 4–17. *The
    foolish shepherd punished, and the flock purified
    through judgment.*

Awake, O sword, against my shepherd, and against the 7

---

4. Such prophets will themselves be anxious to be rid of everything connected, either inwardly or outwardly, with their pro-
fession. The **hairy mantle** was the distinctive dress of a prophet
(see e.g. 2 Kings i. 8 and ii. 13), but had now been used for the
deception of the community.

5. Still full of the spirit of deception, he declares his life has
been one of toil, quite unlike the freedom of the prophet.

6. He attempts a further excuse, in order to explain the
wounds which shew on his breast as he works in the fields. But
the words admit of more than one interpretation. (i) The wounds
are those inflicted by his relatives (see *v.* 3), from whom he has
escaped. As they are on his breast and not on his back, they
cannot be due to blows he has received as a slave, so he explains
with some truth that they were incurred on a visit to his friends.
(ii) The wounds are self-inflicted, after the manner of the prophets of Baal (1 Kings xviii. 28), and reveal him as one who has
indulged in foreign rites. He is forced to confess the truth, saying
that it was in the temples of other gods that he received them.
This explanation depends on the fact that the Heb. word rendered
friends is elsewhere translated 'lovers' (as R.V. marg. here),
and is used by Hosea (ii. 5 ff.) to mean heathen gods. But in
that passage the gods are 'paramours,' not of an individual, but
of the whole people, the spouse of Jehovah, who have played the
adulteress by seeking other lovers. The whole explanation is
somewhat far-fetched, and the former seems preferable. Possibly
the ambiguity is intentional on the part of the cunning prophet.

7–9. It is generally agreed that these verses are out of place,
and form part of the prophecies of ix.–xi. Not only have these
verses no connexion with what goes before and after, but they

man that is my fellow, saith the LORD of hosts: smite the
shepherd, and the sheep shall be scattered; and I will
8 turn mine hand upon the little ones. And it shall come to
pass, that in all the land, saith the LORD, two parts therein
shall be cut off and die ; but the third shall be left therein.
9 And I will bring the third part through the fire, and will
refine them as silver is refined, and will try them as gold

---

form the natural sequel to the allegory of the foolish or worthless
shepherd in xi. 15-17, and describe his fate and the result of his
rule, which was itself a punishment for the rejection of the good
Shepherd. The earlier passage is not complete without this one,
and also it explains why the shepherd is to be smitten in this
later passage. There is no hint of a reason, or reference to a
shepherd at all, in the later chapters.

Jehovah calls on the sword to destroy this unworthy shepherd.
In xi. 17 it had already been said that 'the sword shall be upon his
arm,' but there was no mention of punishment for the flock. Here
they are scattered and their numbers so reduced by their trials
that only a third are left. These have at length learnt their
lesson, and renew the covenant with Jehovah which had been
broken.

7. against my shepherd. See note on xi. 16 for guesses as to
the person referred to. Dr Barnes heads the paragraph 'The
Fall of Zechariah,' but this is only one of many possibilities.

the man that is my fellow: i.e. a fellow-shepherd with Jehovah.
It need not imply (as Driver) that the man is a high-priest.

smite the shepherd, etc. These words were quoted by our
Lord after the Last Supper—Mark xiv. 27, but their connexion
with the worthless shepherd shews that originally there was
nothing Messianic about them. It is noteworthy that instead of
'smite' the N.T. gives 'I will smite.' This reading is found in
some MSS of the Septuagint, and is very likely right, as it
accords better with **and I will turn** in the second part of the
verse.

I will turn mine hand upon the little ones: i.e. in judgment
even on the lambs of the flock. But Dr Barnes says the action is
'for good.'

8. two parts therein. In Ezekiel's description of the judgment on Jerusalem (v. 12), a third part dies by pestilence, a third
by the sword, while the remaining third are scattered. These
words may be in imitation of that prediction.

9. as silver is refined. Similes taken from smelting are frequent in the O.T., cf. Ps. lxvi. 12, 'Thou also hast tried us, like
as silver is tried.'

is tried : they shall call on my name, and I will hear them :
I will say, It is my people ; and they shall say, The LORD
is my God.

(*b*) JERUSALEM, AT LENGTH DELIVERED FROM HER
    ENEMIES, IS MADE THE CENTRE OF THE WORLD'S
    WORSHIP OF JEHOVAH.

xiv. 1–5. *The deliverance of Jerusalem from the heathen.*

Behold, a day of the LORD cometh, when thy spoil shall **14**
be divided in the midst of thee. For I will gather all 2
nations against Jerusalem to battle ; and the city shall be
taken, and the houses rifled, and the women ravished : and
half of the city shall go forth into captivity, and the residue
of the people shall not be cut off.from the city. Then shall 3
the LORD go forth, and fight against those nations, as when
he fought in the day of battle. And his feet shall stand in 4

---

xiv. 1–5. The final prophecy begins with the same theme as
the previous section (xii. 1–xiii. 6), viz. an assault of the nations
on the holy city, and its rescue by Jehovah. But whereas in xii. 2
the city is only besieged, here it is actually taken. Hence the
suggestion that there was a fourth author in these six chapters
(of a more optimistic turn than the third), whose work begins at
xiv. 1. Driver therefore heads the section A⁴.

If the events of xii. refer to the destruction of Jerusalem in 586,
the same is true of the present prophecy. But the fact that this
passage is of an apocalyptic nature, describing unheard-of miracles
as wrought by Jehovah (see Introd. p. 86), makes it doubtful
whether there is a definitely historical element or not. Perhaps
it is enough to say that both in xii. and in xiv. the imagery of
the events is *suggested* by the calamity of 586. *vv.* 1–5 form the
introduction to a fresh picture of the Messianic age.

1. a day of the Lord. This is not so definite as what we mean
by *the* day. More than one such crisis was contemplated.

thy spoil, etc. Evidently Jerusalem is addressed.

2. The terrible possibility of such horrors even in our own day
has been brought near to us.

all nations. The universality of the attack suggests that it is
an imaginary one.

3. as when he fought, etc. Prefer the translation 'as when
he fighteth in the day of drawing nigh.'

4. God's interposition takes the form of an earthquake which

that day upon the mount of Olives, which is before Jerusalem on the east, and the mount of Olives shall cleave in
the midst thereof toward the east and toward the west, *and
there shall be* a very great valley ; and half of the mountain
shall remove toward the north, and half of it toward the
5 south. And ye shall flee by the valley of my mountains;
for the valley of the mountains shall reach unto Azel: yea,
ye shall flee, like as ye fled from before the earthquake in

---

alters the contour of the hills east of Jerusalem. The way of the
Lord is thus prepared, as in the well-known passage in Is. xl. 3, 4.

the mount of Olives. This is the first time that the familiar
name is used for the hill on the other side of the valley of Kidron.

5. There is much uncertainty as to the translation and meaning of this verse. (i) The statement of the R.V. text is that the
inhabitants left in Jerusalem will escape eastward through the
cleft thus made in the mountain, their flight being compared with
the rapidity with which men fled on the occasion of an ordinary
earthquake centuries before. (ii) A trifling alteration of the
Hebrew gives the reading of the Septuagint and R.V. marg. 'the
valley of my mountains shall be stopped.' The meaning is then
that the valley of the Kidron is filled up, so as to make, with the
cleft of *v.* 4, a level exit from Jerusalem. The valley is exalted
as well as the mountain being brought low, for the way of the
Lord. The question remains whether we shall keep the 'ye
shall flee' in the second part of the verse, or follow the Septuagint again in reading 'yea, it shall be stopped, like as it was
stopped.' In this case there is no reference at all to flight, but
simply to an upheaval like the one when the valley was blocked
centuries before 'because of the earthquake.'

In the light of *vv.* 8 and 10, where other physical features of
the country are changed, without any idea of a way of escape
being made, this second explanation is the more satisfactory.
Gihon, the intermittent spring in the Kidron valley, had been
stopped before then in the days of Hezekiah (2 Chron. xxxii.
4, 30).

shall reach unto Azel. Such a place is not known, but is supposed to be a spot either on the Jerusalem side or on the mountain side where the valley began. But the Vulgate rendering,
'usque ad proximum,' has suggested to some editors a translation
of the word, either 'shall reach to the side of it,' i.e. Gihon
(Mitchell, *op. cit.* p. 343), or 'for a valley of mountains shall extend hard by' (C. H. H. Wright, *Zechariah and his Prophecies*,
p. 474).

the earthquake in the days of Uzziah. This took place about

the days of Uzziah king of Judah: and the LORD my God shall come, and all the holy ones with thee.

6–11. *The transformation of Judah.*

And it shall come to pass in that day, that the light 6 shall not be with brightness and with gloom : but it shall 7 be one day which is known unto the LORD; not day, and not night: but it shall come to pass, that at evening time there shall be light. And it shall come to pass in that day, 8

---

the middle of the eighth century, two years before the prophecy of Amos (Amos i. 1). There is no need to suppose that the writer lived near that time. On the contrary, some have thought that the comparison was added by a later hand, and the text of the verse altered so as to refer to flight.

all the holy ones with thee: i.e. the angels. It is easier to read as the Septuagint, 'with *him*.' But Dr Barnes (*op. cit.* p. 101) prefers to take it as a quasi-benediction addressed to Jehovah, i.e. 'All the holy ones be with thee.' This is ingenious, but unlikely.

6–7. After the earthquake, the next divine manifestation lies in a new regulation of day and night. In the absence of powerful artificial light, darkness was one of the horrors of the ancient world, and an apocalyptic future was frequently connected with the absence of night. The promise of Rev. xxii. 5, 'There shall be no night there,' is frequently anticipated in the O.T., e.g. in Is. xxx. 26 and lx. 20, while Amos tells his guilty hearers that they have brought on themselves a terrible reversal of their expectation, even a day of the Lord which 'is darkness and not light' (Amos v. 18).

6. the light shall not be with brightness and with gloom: i.e. there shall not be alternations of day and night, but one steady light. Cf. *v.* 7 'not day, and not night.' But the reading of the R.V. marg. suggests a different picture ('there shall not be light, the bright ones shall contract themselves'). First there is a failure of the heavenly bodies, such as often accompanies an earthquake. This will be succeeded (*v.* 7) by a half light, neither fully day nor fully night. Then when night would normally come on, a new creative fiat will grant the light of day.

7. it shall be one day: either 'one continuous day,' or (if the second explanation of *v.* 6 be adopted) it is merely 'some day, known only to Jehovah.' Mitchell explains 'the day shall be one,' i.e. unique.

8. The chief drawback to the capital was its miserable water supply. That there should be rivers of water flowing through the city was a part of the ideal frequently pictured. It is enough to refer to Ezekiel's vision (xlvii. 1–12) of the waters flowing out

that living waters shall go out from Jerusalem; half of them
toward the eastern sea, and half of them toward the western
9 sea: in summer and in winter shall it be. And the LORD
shall be king over all the earth: in that day shall the LORD
10 be one, and his name one. All the land shall be turned as
the Arabah, from Geba to Rimmon south of Jerusalem;
and she shall be lifted up, and shall dwell in her place,
from Benjamin's gate unto the place of the first gate, unto

---

from the sanctuary over all the country (on which the present
passage appears to be based), and the 'river of water of life' in
the new Jerusalem of Rev. xxii. 1. Here the waters are **living**
in contrast with the rain water on which the city partly depended,
and **in summer and in winter** in contrast with the usual streams
which failed in the hot weather. If the miracle is more than a
physical one, it refers to the spread of blessings from Jerusalem,
but such an interpretation seems unnecessary.

   9. shall...be one, and his name one: in contrast with the
many gods of the heathen world, some of which were called by
different names, and also bore compound titles.

   10. Jehovah has already altered the contour of Jerusalem and
its surroundings (*v.* 4). He now proceeds to do the same with the
whole of Judah, making it sink into a flat plain like the Arabah (the
fertile strip of land on each side of the southern reaches of the
Jordan), while Jerusalem alone is lifted up, and is therefore con-
spicuous from afar. A similar lifting up of Jerusalem had already
been pictured, as in Is. ii. 2, whereby it could be seen afar as
the goal of the nations' pilgrimage. But as the idea of *spiritual*
exaltation entered into the earlier prophecy, it is probable that it
does here also.

   The Septuagint suggests quite a different rendering of the first
clause, 'As the Arabah, so shall he encompass the whole land
from Geba,' etc., meaning that Jehovah will surround the whole
land, the fertile Arabah and the rest alike.

   from Geba to Rimmon. The northern and southern limits of
Judah here seem to be given, though En-Rimmon, mentioned in
Neh. xi. 29, is not so far as Beersheba, the more familiar boundary of the land (e.g. in 2 Kings xxiii. 8). Geba was a few miles
north of Jerusalem.

   from Benjamin's gate, etc. These seem to be the limits of the
restored city. If the words had been written after the walls had been
rebuilt by Nehemiah in 444, they would have been made to fit
better with his restoration. But the promise of the verse that the
city should extend thus, obviously depends on the fact that it had not
yet been restored. It is curious that the actual spots mentioned

the corner gate, and from the tower of Hananel unto the king's winepresses. And men shall dwell therein, and there 11 shall be no more curse; but Jerusalem shall dwell safely.

12-15. *The terrible fate of the nations which had fought against Jerusalem.*

And this shall be the plague wherewith the LORD will 12 smite all the peoples that have warred against Jerusalem: their flesh shall consume away while they stand upon their feet, and their eyes shall consume away in their sockets, and their tongue shall consume away in their mouth. And it shall come to pass in that day, that a great 13 tumult from the LORD shall be among them; and they shall lay hold every one on the hand of his neighbour, and

---

are not known with certainty, but if we take 'the corner gate' as explaining 'the first gate,' they mark the boundaries, first from East to West, and then from North to South.

Benjamin's gate seems to have been the one leading to Benjamin, and therefore must have been somewhat N. as well as E., possibly the sheep gate of Neh. xii. 39.

the first gate: perhaps the 'oldest gate,' or the 'outermost,' in relation to the E.

the corner gate: probably at the N.W. corner, is mentioned in Jer. xxxi. 38 as a spot from which the city should be rebuilt 'unto the tower of Hananel.'

the tower of Hananel: mentioned in Neh. iii. 1.

the king's winepresses. These would be near the 'king's garden,' and the former palace, mentioned in Neh. iii. 15.

11. Readiness to dwell in the capital was by no means manifest in Nehemiah's time (xi. 1, 2). They are now promised that the 'ban' of destruction at the hands of enemies shall no more threaten the city, and therefore men will not be afraid to dwell in it.

12-15. In these verses the record of the relief of Jerusalem is resumed from *v.* 5. The earthquake is followed by plague and panic, then three punishments corresponding with those threatened 'when Gog shall come against the land of Israel' in Ezek. xxxviii. 18-22.

12. The terrible suddenness of an attack of plague, and its horrible effects, are here graphically and almost gleefully described.

13. a great tumult from the Lord. The word used is that of 1 Sam. xiv. 20 for 'discomfiture,' when the Philistines in panic fought against each other.

they shall lay hold, etc. : in order to strike a blow at him.

his hand shall rise up against the hand of his neighbour.
14 And Judah also shall fight against Jerusalem; and the
wealth of all the nations round about shall be gathered
together, gold, and silver, and apparel, in great abundance.
15 And so shall be the plague of the horse, of the mule, of
the camel, and of the ass, and of all the beasts that shall
be in those camps, as this plague.

16-21. *Jerusalem becomes the Sanctuary of all nations.*

16 And it shall come to pass, that every one that is left of all
the nations which came against Jerusalem shall go up from
year to year to worship the King, the LORD of hosts, and
17 to keep the feast of tabernacles. And it shall be, that
whoso of *all* the families of the earth goeth not up unto
Jerusalem to worship the King, the LORD of hosts, upon
18 them there shall be no rain. And if the family of Egypt

---

14. Judah also shall fight against Jerusalem : apparently
not against their brethren (as may have been the case in xii. 2),
but against the city which was still in the enemy's hands. They
will take the city, and so obtain the booty left by the foe.
' **15.** Difficulty has been found in this fresh reference to the
plague, but here we have an extension of it from the men to their
animals.

16-21. The lurid picture of destruction is succeeded by a final
picture in which the remnant of their heathen foes (like the remnant of the Jews themselves in xiii. 7) come up to worship, and
the holiness of the sanctuary spreads over the people and all that
they use.

16. the King : an unusual name, but appropriate to the God
who has proved Himself sovereign over all the nations.

to keep the feast of tabernacles. This was the final festival
of harvest, and was therefore suitable for all to express their
thankfulness. The other idea of the festival was a commemoration of the dwelling in 'booths' during the wanderings. In Deut.
xvi. 16 it is specially stated that the 'stranger' was to take part
in it. For the connexion between this feast and that recorded in
Neh. viii. 16 ff., see Introd. p. 85.

17. Failure to join was an act of ingratitude for the harvest,
and was therefore to be punished promptly by the failure of the
rains which ought to follow a few weeks afterwards.

18. The meaning must be that, although Egypt, which depended on the inundation of the Nile, was independent of rain,

go not up, and come not, neither *shall it be* upon them; there shall be the plague, wherewith the LORD will smite the nations that go not up to keep the feast of tabernacles. This shall be the punishment of Egypt, and the punish- 19 ment of all the nations that go not up to keep the feast of tabernacles. In that day shall there be upon the bells of 20 the horses, HOLY UNTO THE LORD; and the pots in the LORD'S house shall be like the bowls before the altar. Yea, 21 every pot in Jerusalem and in Judah shall be holy unto the LORD of hosts: and all they that sacrifice shall come and take of them, and seethe therein: and in that day there

---

it would be punished all the same, the 'plague' apparently coming to them in a similar way to the rest, through the failure of the needed water. But the reading of the R.V. does not say this, and the marginal note despairs of its sense. It is better to read as R.V. marg., 'shall there not be upon them the plague etc.?' or as the Septuagint and Syriac, 'upon them shall be the plague.'

19. If *v.* 18 contains a question, this is the answer to it.

20. Holy unto the Lord. This was the inscription upon the high-priest's mitre (Exod. xxviii. 36). This holiness is now to be so extended that it shall even be upon the horses' bells. As horses in the O.T. represent war, their connexion with holiness is un-expected, and perhaps promises the ending of warfare. Here they are the horses of the pilgrims, as their riders have now be-come such. Jeremiah (ii. 3) had already suggested an extension of the inscription to the whole of Israel.

the pots...shall be like the bowls: i.e. the caldrons in which the sacrifices were boiled would be as holy as the basins used in the sanctuary for holding the sacrificial blood.

21. This final verse shews that the holiness will extend far more widely still. The thronging nations would not find enough caldrons for their use in the temple, or even in the whole city. Therefore every vessel throughout the land would assume a similar holiness. The spiritual meaning underlying the cere-monial one is that all the people of the land will partake of Jehovah's nature, and will help the pilgrims who come from afar to worship the Lord in the beauty of holiness.

all they that sacrifice: evidently the reference is to the foreign pilgrims, who would be allowed to take the vessels from Jewish households for their holy purpose. The verse may be compared with Zechariah's own last picture (viii. 23) of ten foreigners taking hold of 'the skirt of him that is a Jew.'

seethe therein: i.e. boil the sacrifices.

shall be no more a Canaanite in the house of the LORD
of hosts.

---

there shall be no more a Canaanite, etc. The Canaanites were
the lowlanders, who lived along the sea coast. They were the
recognised traders of the time, and in Nehemiah's time we hear
of 'men of Tyre' coming to Jerusalem with 'all manner of ware'
and profaning the sabbath by selling on that day. Part of their
'ware' would doubtless be temple vessels, so the prophet says
that, when all offer these willingly for use, there will be no need
of ordinary merchants to sell them. This explanation is given in
the R.V. marg. in its rendering 'traffickers.' The suggestion of
a profaning element seems also to be present, which shall no
longer be there when all is holy. This leads on to the thought
of the cleansing of the temple by our Lord from the presence
of the traffickers who were turning it into a house of merchandise
(John ii. 16).

INDEX

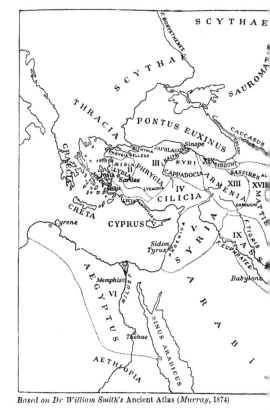

Based on *Dr William Smith's* Ancient Atlas (*Murray*, 1874)

THE PERSIAN EMPIRE AN

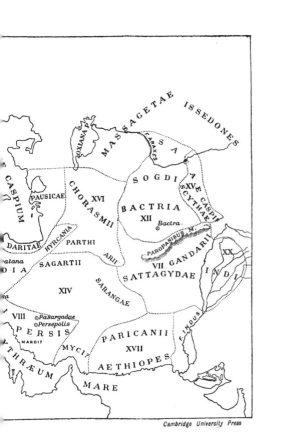

MASSAGETAE
ISSEDONES
ROXANA P.
SACA
SOGDI
ARAXES
CHORASMII
XVI
SACA E CASPII
BACTRIA
XV
SCYTHAE
PAUSICAE
XII
CASPIUM
Bactra
PAROPANISUS M.
DARITAE
HYRCANIA
PARTHI
ARII
XX
SAGARTII
VII GANDARII
...atana
SARANGAE
SATTAGYDAE
INDI
O I A
XIV
...a
VIII
Pasargadae
Persepolis
PARICANII
PERSIS
XVII
MARDI?
MYCI?
AETHIOPES
THRAEUM
MARE

S SATRAPIES, c. 520 B.C.

For EU product safety concerns, contact us at Calle de José Abascal, 56–1°, 28003 Madrid, Spain or eugpsr@cambridge.org.

www.ingramcontent.com/pod-product-compliance
Ingram Content Group UK Ltd.
Pitfield, Milton Keynes, MK11 3LW, UK
UKHW012333130625
459647UK00009B/252